AT THE CORE
of EVERY HEART

Reflections, Insights, & Practices
for Waking Up and Living Free

Dr. Gail Brenner

Ananda Press

Published by Ananda Press

The information in this book is solely for general personal use and education. It should not be treated as a substitute for professional assistance, psychotherapy, or counseling. In the event of physical or emotional distress, please consult with appropriate health care professionals. The application of information in this book is the choice of each reader, who assumes full responsibility for his or her understandings, interpretations, and results. The author assumes no responsibility for the actions or choices of any reader.

Printed in the United States of America

ISBN-13 (paperback): 978-0-9864282-3-4
ISBN-13 (ebook): 978-0-9864282-4-1

Cover and book design by Lorie DeWorken,
MIND the MARGINS, LLC

Author photo by Kenedy Singer

ALSO BY GAIL

The End of Self-Help:
Discovering Peace and Happiness
Right at the Heart of Your Messy, Scary, Brilliant Life

To download the first chapter, please go to
http://GailBrenner.com/email-signup/

To my mother, Grace Brenner
May your memory be a blessing

Contents

"When by the flood of your tears
the inner and outer have fused into one,
you will find Her whom you sought with such anguish,
nearer than the nearest, the very breath of life,
the very core of every heart."
Sri Anandamayi Ma

Introduction

At the core of your heart lies the deepest fulfillment, the most profound peace. How do I know? Just as Anandamayi Ma says, it is what's here at the core of all of our hearts—and you are no exception.

Before the tragic stories that keep us alienated and separate and in the midst of the most gripping whirlwind of emotions, there's the simple fact that everything is truly okay just as it is.

For many years, I woke up every morning with a deep feeling of dread that sat in my heart like a stone. It was a subtle feeling that something was wrong, and it colored my whole day, day after day. I didn't even realize this was why I felt so anxious until I started getting curious about my in-the-moment experience.

I began waking every morning greeting this feeling by saying, "Hello, Dread." I did nothing except spend a few quiet moments acknowledging its presence and noticing how it felt in my body. Then I went on with my day.

A few months later, it dawned on me that I hadn't experienced that feeling for some time. Like a miracle, just by giving it a friendly welcome, it dissolved, never to return again in quite the same way. My outlook was brighter, I was happier, and I felt relieved to not be carrying this heavy discomfort.

Since then, I've met many inner experiences with the same welcoming presence. I've felt fear, pain, sadness, grief, frustration, and anger—the array of emotions that arise in the everyday experience of inhabiting this human life. And each time I meet these, I realize they are not who I am. They always subside, yet something remains—an undeniable aliveness, an alert presence that is calm and peaceful. And when my attention rests here, there's a deep sense that all is perfectly okay.

This book invites you to tap into this undercurrent of pure aliveness, and when you do, you will see your struggles in a whole new light. You don't have to believe you're damaged goods. You don't have to buy into the anxiety that gets your mind spinning in endless worry.

You realize that being defined by these troubles is optional. The alternative is to honor your deepest longing by relaxing into the river of life and the natural unfolding of things. Over and over, you return to the sacred space of presence and a heart boundlessly open to everyone and everything.

I'm delighted to connect with you through the pages of this little book in our mutual love of peace and happiness. The book contains 52 short essays designed to invite your attention back to sanity, ease, and the loving immediacy of this now moment. They welcome you to expand beyond your contracted thoughts and feelings to the infinite spaciousness here right now.

Each chapter includes a practice to experiment with in your own experience. Feel free to follow the chapters in order or skip around to find the ones that draw you in.

But be sure to engage fully with the practices so you can move beyond the busy mind. The peace you're looking for isn't in your thoughts—it's available right here and now, and it's beckoning you to experience it directly.

This book is offered in celebration of the ultimate desire—to wake up and live free. May you know the very breath of life, where we meet as one at the core of every heart.

Love to you,
Gail

March 2016
Santa Barbara, CA

1

Look Within

You won't find lasting peace in the objects of the world. Sure, your life circumstances may be just right for a while, but if you invest your happiness in things that are unreliable—relationships, jobs, money, lifestyle, your health—you are asking to be disappointed.

Relationships end, jobs fall away, and your good health won't last forever. If you rely on these for happiness, what happens when they change? You're left batted about by circumstances with no steady anchor to pull you through.

Instead of looking outside yourself for peace and happiness, make a U-turn with your attention and look within. When you turn your attention away from the objects of the world, what do you look for?

First, begin to become familiar with what you pay attention to in your own experience.

Notice what thoughts grab you. You might find stories you repeat in your mind, judgments and opinions, thoughts about what you want and don't want, and expectations about how things are supposed to be different than they are.

And you'll discover feelings—sadness, worry, frustration, emptiness, joy, anger.

Once you become aware of the experiences that hook your attention, you'll begin to understand why you're not content. How could you possibly be happy if your whole reality consists of anxious thoughts and chronically painful feelings?

But there's something else you notice when you look within, which is that you are aware. When you stop to look deeply, you'll find a stillness, an energetic aliveness that feels incredibly free. It's the gap between thoughts, the ease you experience when you notice feelings rather than being consumed in them.

Explore this space and get to know it intimately, as this is where the treasures of peace and happiness lie.

It was a pivotal moment for me when I started looking within. Before then, it hadn't dawned on me that there was anything else other than me, Gail, this person living in the world who was trying desperately to figure out how to be happy.

Slowing down by beginning to meditate changed my perspective entirely. Instead of playing out my unsatisfying life story, I could be still and watch my thoughts and feelings. I sat quietly and watched the array of urges, dramas, and emotions. What a revelation to realize what was actually happening!

Eventually, I became curious beyond meditation to understand my true identity. I wanted a deeper experience of knowing what's real than just watching objects come and go. And I discovered it in the space of just being aware.

But looking within was the first essential, revolutionary step.

PRACTICE: *Whenever you notice that you're stressed, upset, or unhappy in any way, stop and take a breath. Shift your attention from the outer world to your inner landscape of experience.*

Take a few moments to find the core of awareness, and from here, recognize the thoughts and feelings that have grabbed your attention. Do this over and over both in formal periods of meditation and any time throughout the day.

Don't judge yourself when you realize you've been lost in thought. Simply, gracefully, shift your attention to being aware, and say, "Okay, I'm home." It's a profound celebration of the moment.

2

Tending the Garden of Presence

Just as a garden needs tender loving care to thrive, so does knowing your true nature as aware presence. After all, your conditioned habits run deep. If you're like the rest of humanity, your body is programmed to react with tension and contraction from a very early age, and your thought patterns are so automatic that they've become your reality.

How do you tend the garden of presence? Orient your whole life toward what you really want.

- Have a pile of books by your bedside and read something grounding and inspirational before you go to sleep.

- Slow down enough to make conscious decisions from love and clarity, not conditioning and fear.

- Weed your garden of conditioned habits that separate you from life. What habits, people, or life situations, in your heart of hearts, do you know need to go?

- Be unyielding in your quest to shed false identities and stories that aren't serving you.

- Spend time every day being quiet.

- Stop and check in often to notice if you've fallen asleep in automatic habits and appreciate the return home to presence.

- Enjoy the moments of creativity, peace, wonder, joy, and stillness.

Keep the fire for awakened living burning brightly in you. That's what I continue to do every day. Let it inform how you show up in your relationships, at work, and when you're in sticky situations.

PRACTICE: *Read through the list of actions above that tend the garden of presence. See which ones resonate, and integrate them into your daily life with diligence and joy.*

3

Knowing and Not Knowing

I used to live an anxiety-fueled life that thrived on structure. It was a way of keeping control so I didn't have to face the abyss of not knowing. It sort of worked, but there was a down side. Almost everywhere I turned, I found opinions, judgments, and beliefs about how I thought things should be. And my anxiety spiked when things didn't go according to the plan.

Now I know so much better, and life has become a joy. I love not knowing! I have no idea what's going to happen, who will show up at my door, or what words will flow out of my mouth. I relish in the relief of not having to figure it all out.

If you're interested in the natural life, the real life unfolding in this very moment—not the mind-created, fear-based one your mind has come up with—reflect on the demands and expectations you cling to that box you in. They take so much effort to keep going and ultimately leave you tired and disconnected.

Then do this experiment. Just for a moment, turn off the switch so you can't listen to the content of even one thought. Sounds might appear, but you have no idea what they mean.

- Who are you now?

- What do you know?

- Without the capacity for judgments or expectations, how is your experience of this moment?

Let go of everything you think you know, and take one simple step that goes nowhere except into the full vibrancy of your life. Don't fill yourself with made-up mental gibberish that distresses you. Be an empty vessel for love to flourish everywhere.

PRACTICE*: Take a few hours that you set aside in your schedule to not know what's going to happen or what you're going to do. No matter what your mind tells you, just let things unfold.*

4

Everyday Kindness

I wasn't always kind in my daily life. I was too self-absorbed and caught in my worrying mind. I was sometimes abrupt and not always present to people with my heart open. I still slip into that unconscious way of being sometimes, but I usually notice it quickly.

Now that I'm no longer interested in all that mental ruminating, I'm so much more open and engaged in the world. I'm aware of other people and relate to them with kindness and understanding. I'm a kind driver, always letting the other guy in. And I go the extra mile, which doesn't feel extra at all, to connect with the Starbucks barista, the assistant at my doctor's office, and anyone else who enters my sphere.

I take more time to listen, and I'm so much better at putting fear aside so I can enter a room of people with openness and curiosity.

What is the quality of the energy you bring to your daily interactions? How do you show up? Are you open, relaxed, and available, or are you shut down and preoccupied?

I know what it's like to forget to be pleasant. But try it out, and you will find that simple acts of kindness go a very long way to keep the fire for truth alive in you. They break down barriers and continuously remind you that the underlying source of everyone you encounter is the same—loving awareness.

All it takes is moments of genuine connection by meeting another's gaze, asking questions that show you're interested, being thoughtful and caring. And this applies to strangers as well as those you see every day.

Each act is a heartfelt hello. Be pleasant and kind, and let the effects ripple out everywhere.

PRACTICE: *Take responsibility for how you show up in the moments of your life. Reflect:*

- *How do you meet the people you encounter, situations that happen, your own inner experience?*

- *Are your actions aligned with what you really want?*

5

Deep Listening

Our mental chatter is often so prominent that we don't have the space to truly listen. We're always receiving direction about how to move in our lives, but we're too distracted to hear it. We think we have all the answers. We cloud our thinking with drama and emotional upheaval then wonder why our lives are so out of whack.

All of us have the capacity to listen if we're willing to make the space for it. Recently, a friend of mine said with tears in her eyes, "I know I need to quit my job. I'm exhausted. All I want is time when I don't *have* to do anything. I've been living in the structures of my life for a long time and they've lost their meaning." To me, this is clarity, not complaining. She is finally listening to the still, small voice within.

This voice may appear as thoughts with words, a whisper, an image, or a knowing, full-on, "Yes!" to something you may not even realize you wanted.

Every time you're attentive to what you hear, you're opening to the infinite potential way beyond your personal mind's fear-based ideas. And every time you ignore this guidance, you're turning toward suffering and confusion.

Listening is the first step, and being willing to act on what you hear is the second. Listen to the deepest part of your being that just knows. Then have the courage to let your life unfold according to its rightful plan. You may not always like what you hear, but in your heart, you know this voice is true.

What are you listening to today?

PRACTICE: *Get to know the persistent voice of the limited, personal idea of you that you take yourself to be. It often says, "I want…I need…I don't have…" It's never satisfied and content with things as they are.*

Rather than letting it be in charge, find that inner place of alert stillness and rest here. Have no expectations and no vision of how things are supposed to be. Open to whatever emerges.

6

The Safe Haven
of Presence

If you allow yourself to sit quietly for a few minutes, you'll soon discover that you're just here, sitting and breathing. Sure, there may be a flurry of thoughts that run through your mind, but if you let them float off without giving them a lot of attention, you'll begin to notice space, peace, and a sense of ease.

It's hard to put words to it, but at the heart of every moment, no matter now difficult that moment might be, there's an underlying field of awareness that's capable of holding everything. You'll know it in a moment of quiet when you realize that you feel light and relaxed. All of a sudden, you're not paying attention to the voice in your head, and you're happy.

This space of simple aware presence is always here. But don't take my word for it. Check it out for yourself. Stop, breathe, and be quiet for a few minutes (what we commonly call meditation). You might notice objects, like thoughts, feelings, sounds, and sights. Then shift your attention to the space that notices these objects.

You'll find that it's naturally at ease and free of problems.

Now test it out. Stop in any moment, and see if this aware presence is here. You'll begin to realize that it's always here, which offers an amazing possibility.

This space of awareness is available as your safe haven—always. That means that the unhappiness that is created in your mind is truly optional. When your thoughts have become your reality and the world looks unwelcoming and scary, you can let all that go and turn toward this welcoming presence.

When you've convinced yourself that you're a loser or broken and damaged beyond repair, just for a moment, return to this space that is always here waiting for you to notice.

You don't have to dwell in feeling separate, disconnected, and alone. You don't have to be overwhelmed by feelings. You can always return to the underlying field of presence.

And if you're lost in anxiety, worrying about every possible negative outcome, maybe you can return to the safe haven of pure, welcoming "just being aware."

Every time you re-discover the possibility of simply being, you're sending a message to your unhappy stories that you're no longer interested in them. Every time of re-discovery offers a refuge from the need to solve problems that your mind tells you you have.

It doesn't matter at all that you forget and return. You will get lost in the agitated mind because it's strongly conditioned and grabs for your attention. But the aliveness of your pure heart and fire for peace will guide you. You will wake up to the potential of returning to the safe haven of presence.

And that is a moment of celebration.

PRACTICE: *Sit quietly for a few minutes and breathe. Begin to notice that there's a subtle field of space and ease right here. Experience the aliveness and let that experience deepen.*

This is the peace available to you in any moment. When you're lost in suffering, when you realize that veils of fear and dissatisfaction color your reality, turn toward the safe haven.

Do this a little, and you'll experience a little happiness. Do it a lot, and you'll be filled with ease and joy.

7

Consider Forgiveness

Forgiveness is tricky because there's so much misunderstanding about it. So let's start here: if you're holding onto a grudge about something that happened in the past and you're feeling like a victim of it, something needs to shift or you'll be living this identity forever.

The definition of a grudge means that you're feeling resentment and ill will. And you're probably blaming someone for what happened. These experiences live in you like a cancer, fostering stories of misery in your mind. The grudge takes energy to maintain, and it can't help but reinforce your false identity as separate from others, limited in possibility, and doomed to a lifetime of unhappiness.

If you believe you can't stop blaming, consider this: you are the one who is suffering most. Whoever else is involved is probably not hurt by your grudge nearly as much as you are. And you are the one living as a victim, keeping yourself from the joys of being fully alive.

This was one of the insights that set me free. I had held onto a grudge for decades that occupied a large piece of real estate in my body and mind. One day the light bulb went off, and I realized how much anger and resentment I experienced. In one split second, almost like a miracle, it all dropped away. The emotions were propping up the story, and without them the identity I held as a victim vanished into thin air.

Letting go of the past doesn't give approval to bad behavior, and it doesn't require an apology. Forgiving is a choice you make for yourself so you can be free of the past and available to the peace that's present now. You walk away from the contracted part of you that keeps the suffering going…and you expand into freedom. No longer blaming, you're open to seeing everyone's role with clarity. And your heart opens with compassion to the suffering of all.

PRACTICE*: Forget about the word "forgiveness" and don't involve the other person. The path of freedom is about you, not anyone else. Instead, reflect on the resentments you still hold onto.*

Can you see how they don't serve happiness?
Are you prepared to let them go?
Consider the stories you are keeping alive in your mind. How do these stories affect you?
In this moment, right now, what do you choose?

8

Always Fresh

Familiarity comes only from our thoughts. It's our minds that say, "Oh, I know what that is. I've seen it before." And it's our minds that spin the same old stories that we take to be true.

But none of this mind-created stuff is the absolute truth of our in-the-moment experience. And when we're intimately in touch with this absolute truth, our whole perspective on everything changes.

Things don't recycle themselves. There is no such thing as a recurrence or a repeat. It's only our thoughts that make things seem common, humdrum, or boring.

Reality is timeless, which means that every moment is fresh and new. Whatever is happening now is original. It never happened before and will never happen again.

We might think something is familiar, but it's only our minds that tell us that. Turn your attention away from your thoughts, and things are fresh. You realize you're one with this life force that flows into creating everything.

There is only the seamless unfolding of life that emerges unique to any particular moment. See how wondrous it is?

Knowing this freshness, where are your problems with events that happened in the past? How do you respond to that same behavior someone does that always annoys you? Where are your limited stories about yourself?

Turn off time, and see things with the vibrancy of truth—and you're immediately unlocked. You're experiencing everything as if for the first time, because it is. Unclouded by prior history, your options are now infinite.

Touch into this endless openness, and here you are, not knowing, steeped in wonder and possibility.

PRACTICE: *Study your own experience: what does it take to be fresh in this moment? What needs to be let go of? And what do you notice about "familiar" situations when all the history is gone?*

9

Stillness Beckons You

If we don't pay attention to our minds, they continue to spin at warp speed unchecked. Let all these nonstop minds create the world, and you get a culture that celebrates busyness, complexity, alienation, and the idea that there is more to do than could possibly get done.

The result? We live in feelings of stress and pressure, trying to keep up with all the demands we perceive to be so important.

When people in my family phone each other to ask, "How are you?" The answer is invariably, "Oh, I'm busy." Being busy is the norm, and it's a trap.

We've come to worship doing, while forgetting the glorious possibility of being. Yet, the all-encompassing peace of presence is here as the source of everything. It's infinite, boundless, and not one millimeter away from where you are right now.

If you're longing to know yourself as timeless being, you won't find it in your busy mind. Instead, slow down, stop doing, and create the space for still-ness and silence. Let your mind release into this limitless space. Let the boundaries of your personal self dissolve into the ocean of presence.

Keep holding it all together, and the deepest peace will elude you. Let everything release into still-ness, and you'll know who you are.

It doesn't mean that agitating thoughts no longer appear. But when they do, they're barely clouds pass-ing through the vastness of the empty sky of you.

PRACTICE: *Take time to sit and be still for at least five minutes every day. Whenever you remember throughout the day, take a conscious breath and be yourself—consciousness—infinite, boundless, and closer than you could ever imagine.*

10

You Are Already Whole

Some of us have had a tough go of it in life. We've had experiences, maybe starting at a very young age, that have affected our self-esteem, our relationships, and our ability to succeed in life. We think that if we fix the broken parts of ourselves, we'll eventually feel happy.

But the possibility for happiness is here now. We don't need to wait for an imagined future when things will finally be okay. We can stop searching for the magic bullet that will heal the wounds that seem so real. Why?

It's easy to forget, but essential to remember that *you are already whole.*

Drill down, like a miner searching for gold, to the truth of you prior to any learning. What do you find? You will see that who you are before conditioning—the unconditioned you—is whole, free, light, and clear. This truth has no problems and lacks nothing. No matter how many challenging experiences you've had or how badly you feel about yourself, this state of wholeness is still here. It is who you are.

But if you don't need to be fixed, if you are already the peace and happiness you're searching for, why don't you know that?

Unhappiness is a case of mistaken identity. We take the content of our thoughts to be true and believe that our feelings reflect reality. If we think we're inadequate or too emotional or depressed, this becomes the truth that we live by. We define ourselves by these supposed limitations.

But these patterns mask what's actually true. At any moment, we can let these thoughts float by, like clouds in the sky, and no longer believe what they tell us. Then we realize we're here and present, available to life with nothing in the way. We realize our essential wholeness and know that this truth of ourselves has never been broken.

Finally, we stop searching for happiness and live it fully right in this precious moment.

PRACTICE*: Notice the urge to fix the parts of yourself you believe are damaged. What action do you want to take? What is your usual way of dealing with unhappiness?*

Now turn your attention into your own experience to discover why you're unhappy. You'll notice what thoughts and feelings are grabbing your attention and being made real.

Observe them instead of engaging with them. Then look directly at the observing presence. This is you—already whole.

11

Know How Thinking Works

I used to live my life completely caught up in my mind. An underlying sense of anxiety fed a constant stream of thinking that left me feeling stressed and out of sorts.

Now I know it's not a requirement to live in that stress. I've studied these thought patterns and have found 99.9% of them to be repetitive, negative, and patently unhelpful. They don't support, and they don't bring joy and celebration.

One day many years ago, I was lying by the pool relaxing in the sun, and I decided to experiment. I brought to mind some common, worrisome thoughts and immediately felt physical tension in my body. Then I shifted attention away from those thoughts, and noticed that after a short time, the tension released. I went back and forth between thought and no thought until the lesson became crystal clear. And the lesson was about how much unconscious stress I had been holding onto, probably for decades.

From that moment on, I lost interest in thinking. Many thoughts still come, but if they are critical, agitating, gloomy, or divisive, I dismiss them. Because I don't want to pretend that I'm separate from this amazing life that's here right now.

We take thoughts to be real, but they aren't. What is a thought? It's a wisp of energy with words attached. And when we believe the meaning of these words, the thought becomes our reality. Mixed with emotions like fear and anger, the thoughts seem to have a life of their own. We believe the self-doubt, judgments, and fears about the future.

But thoughts are temporary. They are the mind's feeble attempts to protect and control. Recognizing them and letting them be, we're free of their meaning and the tension they create. And we're here, fully alive in this beautiful, uncontrollable, mysterious unfolding.

PRACTICE: *Get to know the content of your thoughts—not to embellish the stories, but to realize how negative and self-defeating they can be. Feel how these thoughts bring stress to your body.*

Check in to see if your thoughts are actually necessary. Don't pay attention to them and see what happens. You may notice that your life unfolds just fine without that constant, judgmental, complaining commentary. In fact, aren't you more here and alive without it?

12

Questioning Everything

I often stop in the middle of whatever I'm doing and realize that I really don't know anything. I don't know the next word that I'm going to type, who will walk through the door, or even what thought will appear in my mind. Truth be told, I'm completely clueless!

I've come to love drifting in not knowing. It's such a relief that I don't need to know anything, and I'm happy to tell my busy mind that it's okay to be at ease. This leaves me floating in the space that allows answers to arise. It leaves me listening deeply through my heart and body. There's a huge space that opens up when I give up trying to know the answers.

Admitting how much we don't know might be hard or scary. We're programmed from birth to use our minds to figure everything out as we try to feel safe and protected. Thinking that we know gives a sense of control and not knowing feels like one huge threat. What can we trust if we don't know? Where do we stand?

But sometimes it becomes obvious that the most intelligent thing to do is realize we don't know. When we're stuck, when we're wrestling with what to do or we don't know how to move forward, when we're frustrated and reaching to the past or future, it might be time to say in all honesty that we just don't know.

This is a pivotal moment that sets the stage for something new and exciting. *Because then it's time to ask questions.* Without expecting any given answer, we stay in the space of not knowing and listen for whatever comes.

Here are some questions to slip into your consciousness. Choose one that calls to you, close your eyes, and let the question be. Don't rush it. Your only job is to be receptive, curious, and open.

You're now available to the natural intelligence of life that is so much wiser than our personal minds. You're open to answers that are way more fresh and creative than any of your mental ruminating can come up with.

You'll notice that none of these questions starts with "Why." Why? Because the function of the why question prods the mind to analyze, deliberate, and figure out an answer. It takes you into your thoughts and out of the present moment.

Instead, these questions invite you more deeply into what is true, real, and authentic. With no interference (and a bit of courage), you get to finally know what your heart has been aching for all along.

PRACTICE: *Take a few breaths and settle into presence. Choose the first question that jumps out at you, and float the question into the space of awareness. Breathe, rest, and be still as you listen. Notice if you resist what you discover.*

1. *What is most alive in me right now?*

2. *What is life asking of me?*

3. *What can I surrender right now that isn't serving?*

4. *What false beliefs am I taking to be true?*

5. *Can I say, "Yes!" to what's happening in this moment?*

6. *What am I avoiding that is asking for my attention?*

7. *Can I stop, breathe, and simply be aware?*

8. *Who or what am I?*

9. *Can I open to what is present right now?*

13

Emotions Fueled by Love

When it comes to our emotional landscape, most of us get stuck. We love the highs of joy and excitement and the serenity of peace and relaxation. But when it comes to those pesky emotions such as fear and anger, we'd much rather turn away from them than peek in to actually see what's going on.

Emotions taken personally and attached to the idea of an individual self are the ones that feel like you've just stepped on a wad of chewing gum. Regardless of what you do, you're still stuck. Your anger keeps perceived injustices alive, and your sadness settles heavy in your chest. And these unexamined emotions give rise to reactive behaviors that cause turmoil in relationships.

They define you and diminish the possibility for clear seeing.

Emotions are a natural part of life. We are feeling creatures with five senses and bodies that react instinctually to stimuli. But identifying with the story of an emotion that takes up residence in our minds is what brings about suffering. And this is the part that is optional.

What if we were to release emotions from the prison of the personal self? They arise, but they no longer attach to any story. Sensations run through the body, but they're not interpreted as dangerous or difficult. And the energy of the emotion emerges unhindered as an expression of the one loving, compassionate heart. Here's how it works.

Fear is all about limitation. In the face of threat, the body is immediately on guard, not yet acting but fully prepared for fight or flight. What if we let that energy to act run free without the mind's fearful projection about what might happen. "You" step out of the way, unleashing the urge to act without regard to fearful consequences.

If you allow the energy emerging from the one undivided truth without the label or story of fear, what actions would happen? How would you move?

Now, consider anger, which starts with a strong physiological response in the body. Letting the physiology free rein, knowing it emerges from essence that is already whole and complete, how would you roar? Without the story of blame or unfairness—and fueled by love—how does this energy want to move?

Take the loss that's behind sadness, and realize it's not just your loss. Let your breaking heart break open to the tenderness that underlies all things, to the fragility of all forms. And there you find the only true solace, which is the realization of the ever-present, undivided life force, the stable presence that is the source of all.

PRACTICE: *You don't own your emotions, although it might feel like you do. Experiment with intentionally setting them free. Work with any emotion—the one that's here right now, the one that grabs you the most.*

Just for a moment, put aside the stories of alienation and separation. Without denying the emotion's energy, let it emerge through the heart of compassion and love. Simply be aware of whatever arises.

14

The Wisdom of Restraining Yourself

I used to be very rebellious, and it got me into some trouble. In the name of freedom, I felt like I could do whatever I wanted, and I certainly didn't want my autonomy compromised by someone else's rules. (Just ask my parents.)

Truth be told, my willful behavior did not make me happy. It was defiant and resistive and kept me from getting what really served me in some important areas of my life. But I eventually learned that what I was calling freedom was actually rebellion. And what I really needed was the wise exercise of restraining myself.

What we call our unrestrained behavior is most often the reenacting of automatic, unconscious habits. Say you feel angry at someone and have the urge to lash out at them. If you don't pause to investigate the urge, you end up making a remark you are likely to regret when you calm down later. Or say you have the intention to exercise, but, without stopping to think, you act out your desire to eat a bag of chips rather than go to the gym. Is this wisdom...or freedom?

Our lives are filled with conditioned habits like these that we call "living life." Some are benign and others mask our happiness and well being. Do you recognize any of the following: procrastination, passivity, hostility, judgment, pessimism?

Without stopping to restrain ourselves, we stay stuck in the same predicament that keeps us bound and limited. But when we pause before the pattern has us barreling down the road to the same disappointing outcome, there is the chance, finally, to tap into the conscious, desired response.

This is how our self-sabotaging desires themselves become our allies. Rather than wishing to banish them or make them disappear, they signal us to stop and step away from the momentum of the conditioned pattern.

The common meaning of the word restraint speaks to holding back, repressing, and keeping control. The implication is that by restraining ourselves, we relinquish freedom and forgo spontaneity.

In fact, just the opposite is true. Real freedom comes from not being ruled by our habitual patterns that are based on fear and confusion. And real spontaneity arises from the space that remains when the habits are put to rest.

PRACTICE: *Find within yourself the sincere intention to refrain from continuing a pattern of behavior that no longer serves you. The pattern can be anything: eating poorly, arguing too much, criticizing yourself or others, showing up late, smoking. Make a vow to yourself, a true commitment to exercise restraint.*

When you notice the pattern has grabbed you, stop. Pause. Take a breath. Step away from it. Put some space around it.

Then rinse and repeat. Whenever you notice you've been dragged along into the conditioned way of being, stop, breathe, and restrain yourself from moving forward.

Now what? Experience the fresh opportunity to be present with your thoughts and emotions. Be open to this new and unfamiliar place. Let life, not habits, show you the way.

15

Discovering the True Nature of Relationships

Looking through the eyes of the truth of things, there's only one source, conscious aware presence, and everything we see, hear, touch and experience is an expression of that. Although it seems like all kinds of objects populate our world, each one, at its core, is only this loving awareness.

Do you think you're in relationships with other people? In truth, there's no me over here and you over there; there's only this loving presence meeting itself, with no space that defines and separates.

But most of us live in the world of duality, meaning that we believe ourselves to be separate entities, and this is where all the trouble starts. We peer out from our personal island with needs, demands, and desires that are frustrated when things don't go as we so desperately wish they would. We long to truly and deeply connect, but we just don't know how to bridge the gap that distances us from one another.

One of the strategies we try is communication. Somehow we've come to believe that we develop intimacy with others by sharing every feeling and concern. Standing in our personal viewpoint, we're told that we have a right to our needs, and we express them openly. In the name of good communication, we draw the other into "the talk," endlessly processing what happened when an interaction becomes difficult.

Being in relationship holds the potential for our awakening, but not by communicating our personal views. Communication at its best can touch our hearts, but what I've learned, and what I want to share with you, is this. When we don't first investigate our own emotional reactions within, we're likely to bring tension, conflict, and separation to our relationships.

Instead of taking a breath and getting curious about how we've been triggered, we tend to blame, criticize, fight, manipulate, and spend our precious time rationalizing our opinions to ourselves and everyone around us. And believe me, I'm as much a culprit as anyone else.

Caught up in the mind's ideas of right and wrong, we're out there in the relationship space spinning in judgment and confusion, which diverts our attention from our present moment experience.

But how we meet our experience is always up to us. We can continue to feed our conditioning—and friction and divisiveness—or we can make the bold and courageous shift to turn our attention away from the other person and directly into ourselves.

We stop seeing others through the veil of our own pain and instead open to what's actually here. This begins the discovery of the undivided expansive heart that embraces everything.

Our reactions to other people become a beautiful invitation for our awakening. These reactions mirror back to us our personal hooks: what we expect from others, how we assume things should be, and the feelings we've been avoiding.

We see clearly how our minds have made separation seem so real, and we surrender our thoughts and emotions into pure, boundless openness.

Feeling the urge to lash out in anger or judge our children and friends, we let ourselves open to helplessness, fear, or shame. And like a trail of breadcrumbs, we follow our personal reactions back into ourselves, realizing we're the source from which all arises—tenderness and love and not any of these painful stories.

Meeting our own triggers is a cleaning out process that leaves us available to the deepest intimacy with all that is. Then the dance of relationship becomes a joyful celebration.

PRACTICE: *Contemplate what triggers you in your relationships. Then reflect: How do your thoughts divide and separate? Take time to*

discover the needs and demands you project onto the other and how that affects the functioning of the relationship.

Access your natural intelligence by asking yourself what you really want. Let yourself be surprised by whatever answers come and honor them.

Detach your attention from the objects of thoughts and feelings, and gently settle into the loving space of being aware. Inhabit that space fully. Welcome the one who experiences painful feelings and anything else that arises.

What would it be like to relate from love and non-separate reality rather than from fear and conditioning?

16

Attachment Is Confusion

I have made a very interesting discovery. Whenever I have an emotional reaction to anything, I am attached. I'm holding a belief or expectation that a given outcome should occur. I think I need something I don't already have. I want what I want, and in that attachment, I suffer.

I recently spoke with a friend who burns herself out helping others. Need to run an errand or research something online? She'll be the first to volunteer. Of course, she is kind in her desire to help others, but her need to make sure people think well of her is running the show. And in her own quiet moments, she admits to an inner emptiness that never feels filled up.

Simply said, when we make our happiness dependent on people, money, success, possessions, or circumstances, we suffer. Because we give up our precious well being to temporary objects that come and go and things we can't control.

Attachments are sticky. They start with a surge of emotion then mobilize strategies to get what we want and avoid what we don't want. How many of us build our lives around getting attention and love from others, for example? Immersed in our needs, we stop taking care of those painful places within ourselves that are triggered. And we miss out on the simple ease of letting things flow.

Being attached masks a feeling that you've been unwilling to embrace. While you're focusing on trying to get what you're afraid of losing, you're avoiding your inner reactions of fear, sadness, and loss.

The quest for the peace we know is possible invites us to turn the spotlight on our own experience to discover what emotions are hiding out. Maybe you're afraid of being alone or you feel unworthy or inadequate. Give these painful hooks your loving attention. When you open to the feelings and understand how your thought patterns pull you in, they begin to lose their power. You meet your feeling of lack with love and care so it stops defining you.

With careful study and clear seeing, the pain of attachment reveals so much tenderness. Where before you felt frustrated and needy, you know yourself to be one with the unity of all life.

PRACTICE: *Notice where you're attached and how those attachments feed your mind. Make a U-turn with your attention to discover the painful feelings you've been avoiding.*

Be the loving and welcoming presence that invites these feeling into the light of awareness. Isn't this deep acceptance the medicine you've been craving?

17

Valuable:
The Body Temple

Thousands of physical sensations appear and disappear in the body every day and most of them don't enter conscious awareness. Besides the breath after a run and gurgles in your stomach, we don't notice the many tiny tensions and contractions that arise as we react to the world around us.

But these sensations offer a lovely and continuous invitation into presence. Your thoughts pull your attention into your mind, but opening to physical sensations is being directly with what's here right now.

All experiences of emotion carry sensations you feel in your body. When these go unnoticed, a story spins, and you're off and running in an emotional reaction or a programmed way of thinking. And all this unconsciousness sets you up to suffer.

Many people live obsessively in worries about the future. The mind incessantly wonders what will happen and if everything will be okay. And the thoughts roll in wave after wave after wave.

What's missed when worrisome thinking dominates is the landscape of the body and its physical sensations. While the mind is going a million miles a minute, the body is in a vice grip of tension and contraction.

The same goes for other emotions—anger, sadness, frustration, jealousy, shame. Every emotion is somehow expressed in the physical body.

The way to peace, even when strong emotions are present, is to open to all of your experience, including the physical sensations. It's very simple. In a vast field of acceptance, you allow the sensations to be present without resisting them. Wide-open and aware, there's no room for painful stories to take shape.

Many of our conditioned ways of being began when we were very young. Even though the people caring for us may have had the best of intentions, we may not have received the support we needed when we felt scared, frustrated, or confused.

Whether or not we remember what happened in our minds, the body has a memory of its own. If your emotions haven't been welcomed, honored, and allowed to be present, their residue stays deeply held in the body as physical sensation.

The chest may be tight so you don't breathe deeply. Your neck may be knotted, or you habitually contract somewhere in your body, maybe in your hips, shoulders, low back, or belly.

If these sensations remain outside of conscious

awareness, you'll experience strong emotions without knowing why. The sensations hide out in the nooks and crannies of your body creating distorted beliefs and urges you can't seem to control. You'll feel pulled to behave in ways that don't serve your happiness and well being.

The medicine is this: to deeply welcome these sensations into the light of loving awareness.

When I began to lose interest in thoughts and started exploring the body, I was amazed at what I discovered. So much had gone unnoticed! And welcoming these sensations was like a homecoming. Finally, everything could come out of hiding.

While your attention is steeped in presence and you're allowing the physical sensations here right now just to be, you're no longer lost in the content of agitating stories. Welcome these sensations fully every time, and you'll start to notice space and freedom. Your whole sense of how you think about yourself will begin to change as the emotions lose their power. And without them in charge, fresh ways of responding to situations in your life are likely to appear.

You're here, alive and whole, rather than being lost in the imaginary, emotion-fueled world your mind creates.

PRACTICE*: A few times a day, take a few breaths and settle into presence. Rest your attention in the open field of presence and invite in all physical sensations. It doesn't matter if they change or not. Simply allow them to be as they are.*

18

No Complaining

Most unattended minds turn toward the negative. Are you a complainer always looking for what is wrong? Then you're caught in the energy vampires of whining and grumbling.

This one definitely hits home with me. My unchecked mind seems to love to compare and judge, concluding that the people and situations in my life are somehow inadequate. I know it gets tiresome to be with me when that mind is in control.

Complaining thoughts will flourish if you feed them with attention, making them seem undeniably real. But these are stories made up by the mind. If you're interested in happiness, don't take their content as true.

While you're busy thinking about everything that's going wrong, you're missing out on what is already good, right, full of wonder, and perfectly okay. This is what is here and alive right now.

PRACTICE: *Let yourself feel into the separation that complaining produces so you're not deluding yourself about its impact. How does it feel to complain? Can you find the space beyond your negative judgments?*

Then inquire with an open mind: who is this complainer? Where is he or she located? Find the stable awareness that doesn't come and go and rest here. What happens to complaining and the one who complains?

19

Learn from Experience

There is a saying that life doesn't happen *to* you, it happens *for* you. Every moment is here to support the conscious realization of your true nature. It all depends on how you meet what's happening.

If you're closed and defensive, thinking you're right and blaming everyone else, you'll miss the teaching this moment is offering you. If you're unwilling to own your role in a challenging situation, you'll stay locked in your limited personal self forever.

Remember this essential truth: nothing that happens is someone else's fault; it's your golden opportunity.

Many people complain of unhappy patterns recurring in their lives. You keep choosing the same kind of relationship partner who leaves you unfulfilled. You just can't find your passion in life no matter how hard you try. You're trapped in a behavioral habit or addiction that won't lose its grip on you.

If you're stuck, your wheels are spinning. And the longing for freedom invites you to bring something fresh and new to your experience.

Keep relating to your experience in the same old way, and nothing will change. But turn your attention into yourself with great curiosity and openness, and you're ending the resistance that's at the core of your problems.

No longer caught in the story playing out in your mind, you're willing to investigate exactly how you're suffering. Standing in not knowing, you're infinitely open to new insights and behaviors that may emerge.

With a wide-open mind and heart, start with these questions:

- What am I feeling in this moment?

- What stories is the mind running?

- What physical sensations are present?

- What is aware and alive in me?

- What am I taking to be true and real that is actually false?

Be honest about how you contribute to the troubles in your life. Deeply inquire into your experience, and you'll find the perfect lesson tailored just for you. Let the pattern unravel, and live the reality of what remains.

It's the treasure that will set you free.

PRACTICE*: Notice when you're suffering, and turn the mirror onto your inner experience. What is your attention focusing on? What thoughts are you believing? What feelings are present?*

Can you love these thoughts and feelings as they are but not give them power? Say, "thank you" to them, then move from openness, not limitation.

20

Know How You Resist

If you want to be free, get to know how you resist—because resistance divides and separates. When you resist events that happen, your attention is pulled into your mind wishing things were different or trying to make sense of what has occurred.

And if you resist welcoming your feelings, you'll never get to the bottom of your suffering.

Resistance takes the whole of your experience and breaks it into unmanageable pieces. You go along trying to be happy, yet there's some unexplored friction always nipping at your heels.

You've heard that what you resist persists? Here's how it works. Say that whenever you feel the least bit lonely, you pick up the phone to call a friend. You might feel better in the moment because you're avoiding the pain of loneliness, but, paradoxically, you're giving the feeling power. You've defined it as a threat that is dangerous and worth avoiding.

This push against the feeling only strengthens its capacity to haunt you. Rather than going away, it hangs out in the shadows of your awareness, contracting your body, agitating your mind, and diminishing your sense of well being. You can't help but feel anxious and on guard so you don't get too close to the feeling.

Aligning with the reality of things as they are is so much simpler. Instead of panicking when a difficult feeling arises, you say these revolutionary words: "Oh, hello feeling." Instead of spinning in thought, you let go of the mental story about the feeling and welcome whatever sensations appear in your body. More and more deeply, you're the welcoming presence that invites all sensations to come out of hiding.

And you begin to get a taste of true peace. Putting down the fight with what life brings you, you're effortlessly there with everything just as it is.

Get to know how you resist. Whenever the alarm bells of suffering go off, do you overdo it with food, alcohol, or too much activity? Do you avoid, ignore, rationalize, or defend? Even talking about your feelings endlessly is a form of avoidance. While you're talking *about* them, you're not really feeling them.

When you realize you're resisting, consider relaxing instead. Let the boundaries between you and your experience fall away. Rather than wanting your experience to change or feelings to disappear, say, "Yes!" to everything. Let it all come and be.

In the moments of deep welcoming, your mind is uninvolved, and you're liberated from the tyranny of separation.

PRACTICE: *At the end of each day, reflect on how you resisted. What feeling triggered you to avoid? What did you do to avoid? What would it be like to meet your experience directly as it is with a tender heart?*

21

From Unworthiness to Wholeness

Do you feel that you're lacking, unworthy, or insufficient? In my humble opinion, this is a self-identity that is way too common these days. It's a painful story that masks the magnificence of who you truly are.

If this thought pattern seems to define you, know without a doubt that it is false. You may not believe that now, but investigate this story of "not enough" with great precision, and it will collapse on the floor in a heap of confusion.

Get to know how the beliefs and limitations of this story wriggle into your mind and take up residence like an unwelcome visitor who won't leave. Then say goodbye to these lies, and walk into the light of your full potential.

It doesn't matter what messages you heard when you were young. It doesn't matter what mistakes you think you may have made.

Go beyond what your mind tells you, and here

you are, as you've always been, free of lack and inadequacy, pure and alive, consciously knowing your essential wholeness. And when this identity of lack is seen through, you'll find so much space for your natural joy and creativity to shine.

Do whatever it takes. Meet shame with love and understanding. Become aware of the beliefs you hold about yourself and the world and let them fall away. Gloriously be consciousness itself: aware, boundless, and fully alive.

PRACTICE: *What if you forgot that you are unworthy? Just for a second, try turning off the unworthy switch, and experiment with living from wholeness. What would you do? What would you say? How would you feel in your body?*

22

No Other

All 6 billion of us humans on the planet emerge as forms from the same source, formless being. Before there's you and me and this thing and that thing, there's just This—the pure undivided vibration of life that is infinite, alive, and aware. I'm calling it "formless being," but it is not a thing, and this label can't begin to capture its splendor. Because every single thing you see is a reflection of it.

Spiritual teachings tell us that formless being is both empty and full. It's empty of separate objects but overflowing with life as the essence of all. Nothing and no one is separate from it, including you. It, or more accurately, you are limitless and boundless, beyond time and space, and filled with potential outside anything the mind could possibly imagine.

From this perspective, any form you encounter is not truly real. It has a certain apparent reality to it, but its true essence is the same as all, the same as you: formless being. And this is the case for all forms that have ever existed—all emerge from one source.

We could say that you see yourself everywhere. Not yourself as a separate form, but the essence of all forms is the same as the essence of you. No difference, and no separation.

Knowing this, you fall into silence, overcome by love.

See what happens when you take this understanding out into the world. You throw a piece of trash on the ground, and you're throwing it onto yourself. You look at a friend, and you see yourself in her eyes. Everything you touch, see, and hear—one source, all you.

PRACTICE: *Look around you right now, and contemplate the reality of no separation. Let boundaries fall away. In one sense, you're looking out through your eyes seeing objects, but in another, consciousness is meeting itself everywhere, with no inside and no outside.*

23

The Futility of Worry

I used to worry a lot, with floods of thoughts running through my mind wondering how things are going to turn out and what I might be doing wrong. There was a constant commentary in my head that made for some pretty tense and anxious times. I was always on edge, rarely truly relaxed.

This went on for years, but somehow I just knew there was another way. Did I really need to live the rest of my life unable to just be content? I couldn't believe that this was how life was supposed to be.

With the help of penetrating inquiry into my thoughts and feelings and guidance from some wonderful teachers, I began to understand the experience of worry. And I made some illuminating discoveries.

Worry is the mind's form of scary storytelling. These thoughts plant made-up, negative outcomes into a future that doesn't exist.

Do any of us know what will happen before it

happens? No. So worrying thoughts leave us living in fear and negativity about what *might* happen, when the reality is that we *don't know* what will happen.

Here are some common examples.

- If I follow my dream to travel, I won't have enough money.

- If I tell her how I really feel, she'll leave me.

- Maybe this pain in my side means that I have cancer.

Worries like these spin a sticky and complicated web in our minds. By making us focus only on the hopelessness of negative outcomes, we're clouded by anxiety, fearful of the future, and lacking the clarity needed for intelligent action.

Consider each of the examples above, and subtract the fear. Then you make plans to have enough money for your travels, you take the risk of speaking your truth with your partner, and you check out the pain so you know its cause.

How does worry serve? If you realize you're worrying, put the thoughts aside and see if any actions are called for. Then meet your suffering with acceptance and understanding. Realizing that the thoughts are distorted and the feelings aren't actually real brings you back to what's true—you're here, breathing, clear, receptive, and alive. Worry is a form of mind activity that hijacks the potential for peace and happiness.

And letting it be sets you free.

PRACTICE: *Approach your spinning mind with tough love. When you notice the worry energy revving up, stop, take a breath, and say, "No thank you," to the thoughts by shifting your attention away from them. Remember that these thoughts aren't actually helping you.*

Feel into your actual experience in the moment—the vast space of presence with thoughts appearing in it.

This simple shift of attention is revolutionary. It empties the gas tank of your thinking and returns you to the deepest happiness, the most profound sense of peace.

24

How Unhappiness Serves

No one likes to be unhappy, but what I've discovered is that unhappiness serves.

I'm actually grateful for the suffering that comes when I realize I'm believing a story about how things are supposed to be and what's missing that I think I need. I now have an opportunity to understand more deeply how this conditioning works. And I once again realize the possibility of being free of it.

Little by little, these programmed patterns have faded. What used to trigger me before hardly lands. Where I spent a lot of time trying to find solutions to personal problems, now I live in much more freedom and happiness. Once I'm aware that my attention has crystallized in negative and limiting thoughts, it takes no time at all to expand into presence.

When you're unhappy, instead of hating what is happening or wishing it were different, do the radical thing and be present with your experience. If you're still reeling from a difficult childhood or your co-worker won't stop doing that one thing that annoys you, take these as golden opportunities to study how you get caught in painful reactions.

Invite the clarity of conscious awareness right into these challenging thought patterns and emotions, and realize the truth—that thoughts are word forms passing through and emotions are sensations lodged in the body.

Know that you are not these objects; you are the welcoming presence they appear in—and you've never been touched by any of it.

By letting unhappiness serve, you tap into the endless well of peace, joy, and love.

PRACTICE: *Take on an attitude of openness and curiosity toward all of your experience. Don't think that the pain you're feeling shouldn't be here. Instead, bring awareness to wherever you're triggered and let the knots of suffering unravel.*

25

Clarity Beyond the Inner Critic

The inner critic is a cruel and painful form of mind activity. Maybe you judge yourself harshly or call yourself names you would never think of uttering to someone else. Somehow this voice convinces you that who you are is inadequate, lacking, and damaged.

The inner critic offers you a distorted view of reality. Sadly, it mutes your creative potential and keeps you from living your dreams. But you have the key to the prison door. You can learn to work with this inner critical voice so it loses its power to define you. You can shed the skin that keeps you confined to this sad and limited way of being in the world.

The inner critical voice almost always has its roots in your childhood. We sometimes internalize the words we hear from others. Or we conclude we're damaged or at fault because we're too young to understand what's happening. We don't have a way of knowing the truth, so we do the best we can by taking these painful thoughts to be accurate descriptions of us.

This leaves an imaginary hole, which is the sense of the inner child who craves love and validation. Care for that young one by figuratively take him in your arms and telling him you'll give him everything he needs. Let that little girl know you'll always have her back and won't leave her.

Do this often so the inner critic has no room to flourish.

Now turn down the volume on the voice of the inner critic. Assume that what it tells you isn't true, because it isn't. Try acting as if you are already whole and filled up and not needing anything or anyone else to be happy. Because you are.

How would you feel in your body? What would you do or say differently?

Don't identify yourself with the negative and limiting voice of the inner critic. Unveil yourself and be the awareness that's always here, completely unconditioned, prior to any thoughts and all identities. This is you, pure and pristine, and being here, the inner critic has never touched you.

PRACTICE: *The voice of the inner critic may be strong, making it difficult to convince yourself that you are not what it says. So take the 3-pronged*

approach offered here. When that critical voice is loud,

1. *Find the hurting place in you and generously offer the love and care it needs.*

2. *Turn your attention away from the false beliefs in your mind to shed this painful identity. I sometimes say, "Thank you, but there's no way I'm going there."*

3. *Try on a new way of being—acting from the truth in you that is whole, capable, and happy.*

When you see through this fragment of pain, you reenter the world no longer carrying around the ball and chain from your past. Letting that go, you're fresh, unencumbered, and finally free.

26

Unraveling Habits

Brushing your teeth every day and saying, "Thank you" when you receive a present are good habits that are worth practicing. But habits that carry with them a strong emotional response deserve your attention.

Habits like these are constellations of thoughts, feelings, and bodily sensations that occur repeatedly outside of conscious awareness. And they bring agitation and unhappiness to your life experience.

They appear out of nowhere, and suddenly you're pulled into acting out some old behavior that you know doesn't serve you or anyone else. Eventually, you wake up wondering how you got there—again.

Some of the habits I've discovered are: a tendency to say "no" immediately to something new before I contemplate what's being offered; underlying fear of everything—overwhelm, closeness, being alone and disconnected; a knee-jerk tendency to lash out at someone else to avoid what I'm feeling.

If you cling to people because you're terrified you'll be abandoned or you compulsively run up the balance on your credit cards, you're a victim of unexamined forces, and you're not free.

What's amazing is that you're not condemned to play out these habits forever. And the healing balm you need is closer than you could ever imagine—it's your curious and loving attention.

Become an expert in the habits that derail you from ease and well being.

- What triggers the habit?

- What urges do you feel? What is your specific direct experience of these urges?

- What thought patterns appear that grab your attention?

- What emotions and physical sensations are present?

- If you're not playing out the habit, what new options do you have for what you can say or do?

Get to know when the habit occurs so you can spot it easily. Then let it unravel. It's like pulling on the end of a ball of yarn until all that's left is a pile on the floor—completely unraveled. Then it loses its power and you're returned to presence—and to new and creative ways to handle what before felt stuck.

How to do it? Every time you notice the habit, take a breath and make that profound shift of your attention to the space of being aware. Don't feed the story, feel the urges without acting on them, and welcome the sensations that appear.

PRACTICE: *Choose one or two habits that need your loving attention. Bring your attention right into your experience in the moment, and inquire into it using the questions on the preceding page. Then be open to new ways of responding.*

It usually takes time for habits to unravel. Don't feel like you've failed if you notice that the habit returns—this is completely normal. Instead, focus on just this moment…and the next and the next. Each moment of awareness liberates you from the prison of the habit.

27

Wave and Ocean

The vast majority of us humans on the planet think of ourselves as separate entities. We're like scared little robots running around protecting ourselves and justifying our existence—while we're forgetting our true nature as undivided reality, the oneness of all that is the source of everything.

To use the metaphor of wave and ocean, we believe ourselves to be separate waves while we forget that our true nature is ocean. But who we are, at the core, is ocean...vast, formless, and ever-present. Let the wave and ocean metaphor support your realization.

1. The ocean and the waves that emerge from it are all made of water. Although waves seem to appear as real forms, their true reality is and always has been ocean. In their essence, there is absolutely no difference between waves and ocean. Try to take a wave out of the ocean. What happens? It's

impossible. Waves can only exist because they're true identity is ocean.

If you define yourself as a separate entity, contemplate the truth that the essence of you is the same as the essence of everything, which is pure conscious awareness. Yes, you are a form and you may play in the world as if you were separate, but in the deepest understanding of reality, you are consciousness itself, the formless source of all.

2. *All* waves are ocean and were never anything but ocean. Not only are you consciousness, every form that's ever existed is also consciousness. Look at everything around you. Yes, it's you, pure conscious awareness. You can't be one millimeter away from yourself.

3. Each wave is unique with a particular character. The universe is so diverse! Look at all the forms of all kinds—not just the variety among people, but every single thing. Amazing! Feel absolutely free to celebrate your uniqueness. And do it by freeing yourself from the conditioning you hold onto that separates and limits you.

4. Waves are temporary, but ocean is eternal. Each wave appears and disappears, but conscious awareness has never not been the fundamental ground of being. This means that all forms will degrade and die, but their essence is unchangeable and

eternal. Relationships, emotions, material things, you, others—all objects disappear, but their fundamental truth remains.

PRACTICE: *Digest each of these points. Contemplate them. Immerse yourself in them fully. See how they apply to your own experience. What is it like to be a separate wave? What is it like when you realize you're ocean? How does this understanding inform your everyday experience?*

28

Effortless Happiness

Your true nature is happiness. And if that is not your experience, then you're believing the mind's voice about who you are and what's not possible for you. You're steeped in fear, whether you're aware of it or not. You're distracted from knowing what is true and real.

Holding up the belief in the separate self takes more effort than you probably realize. When we cut off parts of our experience—painful feelings, truths we're afraid to admit to—we create complexity that needs to be managed.

A friend of mine fears rejection and therefore doesn't tell people the truth about certain aspects of her life situation. This choice yields to another level of fear—that her deception will be discovered. She finds herself swirling in worry and confusion, trying to keep it all straight. The stillness of being seems a million miles away.

If happiness is our true nature, if it's here effort-lessly, then where is it? As we peel apart these personal beliefs, fears, and urges, we start to glimpse the peace that's possible. Rather than taking what we think and feel as real, we discover the simple experience of thoughts and feelings coming and going in conscious-ness. We no longer take them as personal to us.

No matter how much our attention is glued to stories, the reality of loving aware presence is always here at the heart of every experience. And when our attention rests here, we welcome what arises with a full and open heart.

Where before we were agitated and stressed, we're now effortlessly peaceful and happy.

PRACTICE: *At the end of the day, celebrate the times when you've been content and reflect on where your attention got pulled into conditioned habits. If there's any residue of disturbance, let it be present in the space of awareness.*

Give up the fear-based effort to hold everything together, and just for a moment, relax. Inquire: what does it take to experience effortlessness?

29

Your Generous Heart

For most of my early life, I walled myself off from people. I desperately wanted to connect, but those who tried to come close found edges everywhere. I didn't make it easy for them.

As I write this now, it feels like I'm talking about someone else's dream. I know that's how it was, but that frightened and protective "me" is long gone. She was never real in the first place, and now her story is barely a whisper of a memory.

As that story has fallen away, what remains is an open and generous heart, and it's not mine. It's the one compassionate, infinitely accepting heart that's expressed through any given individual form.

It's what has always been here right in your core, waiting for the chance to express itself fully. It just needs to be uncovered.

Our natural state is openness. Seeing that personal identities are false, we're simply here and alive, available and receptive to all that is. There's no separate self we need to protect or defend. Walls are unnecessary, and we can stop pushing people away with demands and neediness.

When the edges started to soften, I felt like the tin man in the *Wizard of Oz*. Almost like being reborn, I had to get used to openness in my mind, body, and heart.

It was creaky at first, but eventually melted into the sweetest surrender. I found that being open was completely natural. It was so relaxing to just be.

With the conditioned me out of the way, there is space for true empathy and caring. Finally, with no personal agenda to defend, love flows freely.

PRACTICE: *In your own quiet moments, let fear subside. Feel into your naturally generous heart and how it wants to move. Give out to others what you think you are lacking. Experiment with going through your day open and accessible.*

You'll notice the urge to keep yourself separate, but let that be. See what new and unexpected ways of being appear.

It may feel awkward at first, but don't let that deter you. Step out of your programming and meet each moment fresh and full of possibility.

30

Are You Willing to Leave Your Comfort Zone?

We humans love familiarity! We'll stay with what's comfortable, even if we're mired in unhappiness, so we don't need to face that scary unknown.

Without understanding why, we end up repeating the same unsatisfying patterns in our relationships, choosing partners we'll never be happy with. We travel through our lives assuming we'll be hurt, rejected, or abused, which only sets up a self-fulfilling prophecy in which all of those things actually happen. We choose addictions that wreak havoc on our lives rather than peek into the painful feelings behind them.

So my question for you is this: is your comfort zone really that comfortable?

Yes, it may be familiar, and you may feel like you have some control because you know what's going to happen. When you're in a groove that you know, you feel safe.

But if you're interested in being happy and fully alive, if you're tired of fighting what is, then consider leaving your comfort zone. Only then can you experience reality without the veil of your expectations and programmed behaviors.

Try stepping away from familiar ways of being. No longer constricted by the past, you're fresh, alert, and innocent. Like a child, you're filled with wonder because everything you experience is new.

I remember arriving in Kathmandu many years ago on my first trip to Asia. Riding in a van from the airport to the hotel, I realized I had just landed way outside my comfort zone. My senses were bombarded with new sights, sounds, and smells. To be honest, it was too much to take in, and I closed down.

But I soon discovered the beauty of being completely open to these new experiences. And I delighted in adventures way beyond anything I could have imagined.

When you leave your comfort zone, the body and mind might rebel like mine did. But here's how to work with that: invite openness in fully.

- Imagine space in your brain for new connections and pathways.

- Let your body feel uncomfortable and unfamiliar as you explore new realms of experience.

- Be so receptive that there's no division between you and whatever you're experiencing.

- Don't pay attention to the mind's judgments and fears.

We can resign ourselves to same-old, same-old and stay on the limited path of the known. Or we can take the plunge and step away from our comfort zone with eyes wide open, unencumbered, available, light, and free.

PRACTICE: *Have an honest talk with yourself about where you're settling for comfort. Is comfort serving you? Experiment with stepping into the land of the unfamiliar where you don't know what will happen.*

See things freshly; be open to new ways of responding. Feel the shifts in your brain and body.

31

Befriending Fear

At the core of almost every problem you'll ever have is fear. So it's wise to make fear your friend. If you read popular self-help literature, you'll be advised to conquer fear, vanquish it, and turn it into an enemy that stands in your way.

But there is a gentler, more harmonious way to approach fear, and it involves learning to *work with* the experience of fear. Fighting fear only reinforces the problem. Welcoming it in love defuses its pull on you. You see how it tangles your thought processes, and you let the thoughts be. You notice how it agitates your body, and you invite the layers of sensation into awareness.

Wouldn't you love to understand how fear works so it's not in control? Wouldn't you enjoy clarity of mind that supports rather than limits you?

There's no need to get rid of fear to be free of it. You only need to recognize it when it appears and know that it can't possibly be the truth of you. Fear will tell you that you're incompetent, you shouldn't step out of your comfort zone, and you'll fail if you do. It loves to tell scary stories that crush your potential and keep you thinking you're small.

But this is the pretend voice of the separate self that thinks it knows how to keep you safe. It paints a picture of a negative future, certain that it knows bad things will happen—when the truth is that it can't possibly know.

I come from a well-meaning family that carries a legacy of fear. My father would often say, out of care and concern, "Don't stretch yourself," and my mother would end phone conversations telling me not to do too much.

Now, I don't want to hurt myself by overdoing it, and like everyone else, I appreciate down time and a break from doing, but the message I got was to stay limited so I don't branch out into that scary territory called the unknown.

When we put fear aside and stop buying into its projections into the future, we realize we're here in presence. It's the unlimited space of now filled with potential. Instead of abiding by the scary voice of fear that shuts down possibilities before we even get going, we're available to the magic of life far beyond whatever the mind could come up with.

When I realized how much fear was driving me, I learned to recognize how it shows up in my thoughts and in my body. I became calmer and more relaxed, able to flow with the rise and fall of my life experience.

Gradually letting it be, I could now step forward open and free. And I love that life is right here, guiding this life form (me) every step of the way into who knows what?

PRACTICE*: Get to know the scary stories fear tells and how it feels in your body. When you feel afraid, take some time to reflect by asking these questions:*

- *What is fear saying?*

- *What if the content of these thoughts weren't true?*

Step away from the grip of fear, and see what life wants to offer you.

32

Staying When It's Hard

How often do we get the urge to run when things get difficult? I know that urge well. In a yoga class the other day, I held the Warrior II pose for what seemed like an hour, and it wasn't easy to stay, let alone open fully to all that was happening.

But I did. There was intensity, lots of sensation, and a kindness in the moment telling me not to pay any attention to my mind that was trying to put up a fight.

If you compulsively do anything—keeping busy, cleaning, using substances, shopping, socializing—you're running from some emotion you don't want to face. Or maybe your way is to retreat into a fog where you dissociate from the full reality of the moment. Either way, you're running, not staying.

Avoiding only keeps us stuck in our habits, acting on unconscious urges, and disconnected from ourselves—and from love. We pretend our emotions aren't present. And we're so distracted by our efforts to resist that we miss out on the opportunity to know the deepest peace.

There is great value in staying, no matter what. We get to experience life! This is what's here—not what our minds wish were here. And when we stay, we immediately stop the momentum of whatever habit is trying to take control.

Staying isn't white-knuckling it, just waiting for the difficulty to pass. It's staying in an open, curious, easeful way—even with the urge to run. Our attention expands into the beingness that supports everything, and we're just here, experiencing, allowing, welcoming.

We realize that turning away only breeds more suffering. We know it's fruitless to try to change anything, and we surrender into the flow of things as they are. Staying is revolutionary in our culture of distraction. Stay, even when it's hard, and you're opening the doorway to intimacy with all.

PRACTICE: *When you notice the urge to run, hide, and avoid, consider staying instead. Take a breath and open to what's real right in this moment. Don't look for anything to focus on or think that you're doing it wrong.*

Simply rest your attention in presence. Just be and stay, no matter what appears.

33

Be Empty of the Exhausting Story of "Me"

An unexamined mind is a self-centered mind. If you're unconsciously taking the content of your thoughts to be true, then you're fully engaged in the story of me…me…me.

If you run on automatic, without realizing it, you're constantly thinking about what you need, what you want, and what you should or shouldn't be feeling. The "I" that you define yourself as is the reference point for everything, and all your thoughts are about your personal agenda.

- Am I okay?

- Am I getting what I need?

- Am I doing the right thing?

- Am I safe?

- I want more.

- I think he shouldn't have said that.

- In my opinion, she should be doing it differently.

- It's her fault, not mine.

Not only is this inner self-talk exhausting, it creates an agitated, unhappy mind. If you identify with the contents of that mind and it becomes the sole focus of your attention, you will undoubtedly feel agitated and unhappy.

Instead of engaging with a mind filled to the brim with personal thoughts of fear and dissatisfaction, consider the radical proposition of being empty.

What if you were to empty out these personal thoughts? How? Take them in a big heap and put them aside because they're not serving.

And here you are, pure and pristine. A mind infinitely open like the sky. Breath breathing itself.

You might think you need a personal self with all of its preferences and opinions. But here's the truth: you don't. Life goes along just fine whether or not the mind is chattering. And when you're empty of the personal self, your experience will be so much more peaceful.

Next time you're lost in suffering, realize how much your attention is supporting the story of me… me…me. Subtract the "me" and all that goes with it, and you're one with the seamless flow of life.

PRACTICE: *Become very familiar with the story of the separate self and how it wends its way into your mind and body. Then empty it out. Pour out the personal needs and strategies that aren't serving. Throw away the needless opinions, demands, and expectations. Then experience yourself as fully here and available to life's unfolding.*

34

The Power of
a Conscious Breath

If you're going to find release from the prison of automatic programming, you need to stop and be conscious of what's happening when the programming is in control. There's no magic to it. We stop, realize the momentum of the conditioning, and stay in presence so we can respond with awareness.

This is where a conscious breath can be very helpful. In fact, often in the moment when we "wake up" from conditioning, we naturally sigh. It's a beautiful sigh that speaks to release, relaxation, and the giving up of suffering.

It's a tender sigh that holds compassion for the imagined one who suffers and rejoices in the ever-present possibility of peace.

This conscious breath is so powerful because it completely changes our physiology. We move from the contraction of stress, that fight-or-flight reaction that keeps us vigilant, guarded, and ready to defend, to expansion and space.

When we breathe mindlessly, we use a fraction of the volume of the lungs. It's enough to keep us physically alive, but we're not *here* in our full vibrancy.

A conscious breath says, "Yes!" It opens our constricted chest and belly muscles. It invites our ribs to move freely. And it welcomes the whole nervous system into the deep embrace of presence.

Why not try it right now? Breathe in through your nose, feeling the chest expand. Don't stop until air fills the lungs from top to bottom. And notice that the breath circles 360 degrees around your whole body. Let the chest, sides, and back of the body expand fully. And exhale with ease.

Now try it again, slowly inhaling and slowly exhaling. Let the breath open tension hiding anywhere in your body—behind your eyes, around your neck and jaw, and in your shoulders and back.

Awareness of breathing is a lovely gateway into the ground of being.

PRACTICE: *Take a few conscious breaths any time you think of it, but particularly:*

- *When you're aware of feeling anxious*

- *When you realize you've just been gripped by a wave of conditioning*

- *When you feel confused*

- *When you feel physical tension in your body*

Let the breaths relax your body and slow your spinning mind. Then shift your attention to re-discover the space of simply being aware. Here, you're alert, alive, completely calm, and perfectly at peace.

35

Feeling Shame and Regret?

It happens to all of us. We convince ourselves that lying is the best option in the situation we're in. We choose actions that negatively impact others. We're unkind and self-centered with those we love the most.

And when we realize what we've done, we're filled with shame and regret.

Some of us even drop down into a seductive hole of remorse where we live for a long time, separating ourselves from the aliveness of life.

A friend recently related about that sinking feeling she felt when she realized how her actions affected others. She could not stop the story, "If only I hadn't done that. If only I had given it a second thought before I acted."

It's a form of self-flagellation that all of us know well, and it's easy to get lost in it.

But instead of flailing around feeling terrible about ourselves, let's take a different approach. It's an approach of taking responsibility, of owning your part in what happened. And it's an approach of love that releases shame's hold on you so you can once again live fully.

First, make amends—a lot. From a place of clarity and tenderness within you, say you're sorry, acknowledge how your actions impacted others, and tell them you'll be using this situation as a learning experience for yourself. And reassure them as much as necessary.

When we betray others, we lose their trust, and it takes time to regain it. We need to show up in love, in openness, and in humility, resolute in our desire for restoring peace. Listen to what others need to say without getting defensive. Courageously meet what's arising within and before you.

Next, peer deeply into yourself to discover the root motivation for the choice you made. You will find fear and need in some form. Name what you needed—attention, approval, freedom, excitement, peace—and discover the fear in you—of boredom, intimacy, authenticity. Notice the thoughts that try to justify and defend your actions.

Now, meet those strategies of the separate self with the deepest acceptance. See them not as you, but as part of the foundation of the false identity you take to be true that keeps you empty and lacking. And meet the pain of others with relentless understanding.

Imagine sitting as part of the audience in a theater watching the drama being played out in front of you. Even though it might capture your attention, recognize that there's a part of you that's untouched by it. Be this uncompromising peace.

Life sometimes shoves learning opportunities our way. It drops them at our feet in a mangled mess, saying, "Here. Take this." And it is up to us what we do with them.

Even the most challenging circumstances serve when we untangle our reactions in the light of conscious awareness.

PRACTICE: *Whenever you experience shame and regret, relax away from the turmoil and become aware. Be fierce in your desire for resolution by making amends and learning even more deeply how your conditioned patterns run through you. Begin to inquire:*

- *What feeling propelled me to make the choice that I'm now regretting? What story got created around this feeling?*

- *How does the feeling live in my body?*

- *Can I find the field of awareness that's not touched by this feeling?*

- *Can I welcome the feeling with love and acceptance?*

When acting on unexamined emotions complicates your relationships, bring awareness to your present moment experience. Make things right with others as best you can. Then discover what hooked you, and let the knot of conditioning release into freedom.

36

One Source

If you peel away the layers of programmed habits that flatten your aliveness, you will find your inner radiance shining brightly. Nurture this radiance, and you will see it reflected everywhere. Why? Because the veils of illusion fall away and you discover the source of everything, the all-pervasive, formless ground of being that gives rise to all forms.

If who you really are is not a separate person with a name, gender, body, and roles in life, then neither is anyone else. Rest in your true nature as pure being, and you'll find that you see through to the same true nature in everyone and everything you encounter. All emerges from the one undivided, non-separate source.

Settling in here, you realize there's nothing to protect, defend, or control. Your heart opens endlessly with love and understanding because everywhere you turn, all you see is yourself.

PRACTICE*: Even if it doesn't feel true to you, experiment with being who you already are, the one source at the heart of everything. Consider that everyone and everything you encounter is somehow you. They may not look like you on the surface, but their fundamental nature is the same—formless being.*

What is your experience? How do you treat people and objects? What if you look in the eyes of "another" and know there's no separation and no distance? How do you feel moved to act in the world?

37

Living the Yes! to Life

I've spent a lot of time investigating how to not suffer, and here's what I've discovered. We can't control what thoughts appear, and we don't have much to say about the events that happen in our lives.

But we do have control over how we relate to what arises. We can resist, blame others, ignore and avoid. We can put our heads in the sand or get passive and give up. We can hate what's happening.

Or we can say, "Yes!" Yes, this is what's happening. This is the reality of right now, and how am I going to move forward from here? How can I relate to this precious moment with ease, grace, and intelligence? Can I meet my emotions about whatever is happening with love and understanding?

I recently corresponded with a friend who was reeling after her partner ended their relationship. She told me how much she had invested in their time together and went on about his fears of intimacy. She was in a great deal of emotional pain, wanting desperately for the situation to be different.

She was being very nice about it, but still she blamed him for not dealing with his fears and allowing the relationship to be all she thought it could be. And she was stuck in heartache, not wanting to accept the facts of the situation.

I suggested that she begin to take in what he said at face value—that he didn't want the relationship to continue. Yes, it's painful, but that is what is true.

And once she says, "Yes!" to the truth, her healing truly begins. The blame stops and she can turn toward her own experience, welcome in her feelings of sadness and loss, and reflect on how and why she wasn't always honest with herself. Yes! is the path to getting unstuck, the path to freedom from suffering, and the way to allow what happens to break through our attachments.

Saying "no" to our experience feeds the anxious, ruminating mind and shuts us down to life. We sleepwalk through on automatic with our heads in a fog, endlessly chewing on ideas about what is wrong with things as they are and how they should be different. Saying "no" leaves us feeling alone and separate, wondering if this is the best that life can offer.

Instead, consider migrating into the land of Yes. With our hearts wide open, we say a full-bodied, unapologetic, thoroughly honest "Yes!" to things just as they are. We might have to meet challenge and difficulty, but it's the only way to find relief from suffering.

Then we get to live! We feel the juiciness of the human experience and at the same time know that we are free. No longer resisting the facts, we're finally open to flowing with the timeless natural unfolding of life.

PRACTICE: *Become an expert in how and when you say "No" to life. What do you resist? How does it feel in your body? What are the effects of resisting?*

Now tiptoe into the land of Yes. With all blinders off, say, "Yes!" to the situation as it is. Meet your direct experience with the most loving heart. Use the truth of things as they are right now as your starting point for moving forward.

38

Seeing Through Stress

We all know the feeling. The body tightens, the jaw clenches, and the mind starts going a million miles an hour about all the things that need to be done. We're overwhelmed, and we wonder if we can get it all done. This is what we call stress.

Sometimes stress serves. If you run for exercise, you're putting an extra load on the heart that strengthens it. And you're inviting endorphins to flow through the brain to promote well being.

But if you're chronically behind and pressured for time, or if you're constantly wanting things to be different, you're caught in the grip of a programmed pattern that deserves your investigation. Stress may be natural to the physical body to prime you to act in the face of threat, but when your mind gets involved, creating panic and frustration, you've identified as separate—the one who can't catch up, the one who is overwhelmed, the one who views the world as just one big to-do list. You don't need me to tell you that this is a challenging way to live.

I'm an expert on feeling stressed. By nature, I'm a doer. I like to feel that I've accomplished something valuable at the end of the day, and this sets me up for stress. I so easily expect that I can do more than is possible.

Stress isn't caused by the world out there. It lives in the expectations we've created in our minds for how things should be. And these thoughts trigger our nervous systems to be hyper and on edge. Stress keeps us jumping into the future while we miss the opportunity to be present now.

This is actually very good news. As we see with the eyes of clarity, stress is defined by temporary objects like thoughts and physical sensations that come and go. This means we can choose to grab onto them and let them create our reality—or not.

Imagine yourself standing on the platform at a train station, and the stress train approaches. Out the windows pour those seductive thoughts: "I need to get this done." "I'm behind and I need to catch up." "What if I can't complete this today." And you know that each of these thoughts brings tension to your face, neck, and gut.

You know what it's like to jump on the train, and you're off and running, feeling out of control. But what if you stayed? What if you took a deep breath, rooted your attention right where you are, and let the train pass on?

It doesn't mean that you actually do more—or less. *But the way you approach what you do changes completely.* Without the nonstop commentary about what you should and shouldn't be doing, there's space, stillness, and clarity.

Maybe you need a few more minutes of quiet time to yourself. Maybe things don't need to be as perfect as you think. Maybe you can enlist the help of the people you live with.

I choose sanity over stress because I want to be present for life. And you can, too. Don't believe your thoughts that tell you that's not possible for you, as that's only your stressful mind talking.

Notice the thoughts that derail you from happiness. Bring the space of awareness to the tension in your body. And make the practical changes that support your awakening.

PRACTICE: *Here are some questions to inquire into your experience of stress. Take your time with each one, in space, stillness, and clarity.*

- *What is the thinking behind your experience of stress?*

- *What practical changes can you make to support the release from stress?*

- *Do you resist moving through stress? Do you think stress serves you?*

- *Can you ease into the natural flow of life?*

39

Don't Follow Your Feelings

I know what it's like to live a life driven by emotion, and believe me, it won't make you happy. Someone shows up late, and you're angry. You get some negative feedback, and you sulk in sadness. You live in anxiety, chewing on thoughts about what will happen next and if it will all be okay.

It's like you're a yo-yo on a string, with your happiness tied to all the circumstances in your life that you can't control. If you ask me, this is no way to live.

So what's the alternative? Bring loving, spacious awareness to your emotions. Get curious about them. Know them intimately so they lose their power to control your every move.

Until you become fully aware of your inner experiences, emotions will rule. They're highly conditioned reactions that take up residence in your body, mind, and heart. They're so automatic that you're in deep way before you realize it.

Out of the blue, a memory gets triggered. If you don't catch it, you're immediately consumed in a cloud of sadness and frustration that can color your whole day...and life.

And the effects of feelings ripple out.

If you make decisions based on unexplored emotions, you're unlikely to be happy and fulfilled. You feel empty and choose the first potential partner who comes along, even though the red flags are flying everywhere. Because you're afraid, you don't reach out to engage fully in the world. Your resentment keeps your heart closed and your relationships stuck year after year.

Shining the spotlight of awareness on emotions changes everything. Instead of avoiding or trying to change your feelings, you become aware of them. Then, amazingly, you realize you don't need to follow them into chaos and confusion.

You can follow the truth speaking through you that is in harmony with all of life.

Get to know how feelings move in you so you can learn to spot them.

- What triggers you?

- What repetitive story runs in your mind?

Difficult feelings are like old friends who have overstayed their welcome. You're used to them being around, but you don't really enjoy their company.

Know this, in your heart of hearts: Feelings are temporary, and you can let them go. They don't have to guide and define you. Moment after moment, you can find the place in you that is free of emotion. And when you do, you'll live there happily with clarity, intelligence, and love.

PRACTICE: *When you're caught in a problem or struggle, go right to the feeling that is causing the trouble.*

Take a look at the big picture so you can see how the emotion isn't serving you. Is it fear or anger? Sadness or jealousy? Is it helping or hurting?

Acknowledge the feeling, welcome it, and breathe into the space around it. And when you're ready, bundle it up and place it to the side. Experience your body free of the weight of the feeling and your mind no longer entangled in thinking.

40

The Ultimate Choice

In any moment, we have the ultimate choice, which is where we place our attention. And this means something very important: we can choose whether we suffer or not.

If we're unaware of where our attention is going, we live like robots, playing out habits based on unexamined assumptions and other distorted ideas. Then we wonder why we barely feel alive in our lives.

Say that you have a persistent thought pattern in your mind that criticizes your every move. It squashes your dreams and makes you believe that you're not cut out to be happy. And sometimes the language this thought pattern uses is painfully harsh.

If your attention is drawn into these thoughts, you'll probably feel inadequate, depressed, and woefully limited in the possibilities available to you.

But here's what's amazing. Even though you might not realize it, you do have a choice about where you place your attention.

Once you become aware that your attention is consumed in the content of these negative thoughts, you can start to break the habit by observing them. Instead of believing these thoughts and making them your reality, you become the witnessing presence as the thoughts come and go.

And as the witnessing presence, the watcher of the thoughts, you see them appear, but you realize you don't have to give them your interest and attention. You don't have to make them real. Your attention rests in being aware, in the unfolding of the moment, rather than being stuck in your head believing ideas that only hijack your happiness.

Do this enough, and you'll notice that this "being aware" experience is peaceful. Negative thoughts might be present, but the "being aware" itself isn't negative. It's not harsh, critical, or sad. It's just here, with everything unfolding in it. It's like you're the ocean knowing that waves are arising and dissolving, but they don't affect you.

And when you stop paying attention to the chattering voice in your head and you're just aware, your whole idea of yourself starts to shift. You begin to consider that maybe these ideas that you've taken to be you don't actually define you. Maybe you don't have to wear these limited identities that your mind makes you believe are you. Take them off, and here you are, happy and peaceful.

The first time I realized why I was suffering—that my attention was completely lost in painful thoughts and feelings—it was a huge and exciting revelation. It took some time, but more and more my attention was drawn away from these limiting structures and into the experience of just being aware. Losing interest in ideas about myself revealed the deepest sense of happiness and well being.

PRACTICE: *Learn to recognize why you suffer by noticing where your attention goes. Then notice the "being aware" itself. Eventually, you'll be able to easily choose awareness, and when you do, you're choosing peace and you're letting peace choose you.*

41

There's Space for That

As I write this, I'm grieving the death of my mother who passed away six weeks ago. That familiar sense of steadiness that I always experience as I move through life has been present, but it's been interspersed with times of sadness and just plain emotional pain.

In recent days, I've realized that I haven't given these emotions much attention. I haven't pushed them away, but I haven't welcomed them in either. And I know they've been sitting there humming in the background, muting my usual zest for life.

I talk a lot with others about embracing all of our experience and not resisting anything. I know in my heart of hearts, and through my own experience, that avoidance sustains suffering and embracing brings peace. So I thought it's now time to follow my own suggestions. That means letting down any barriers that have been keeping my emotions at a distance and inviting them fully into the field of conscious awareness.

I led a meeting called *Living in Truth* the other night where a woman described how she had recently been experiencing a lot of emotional turmoil. But during the guided meditation, things quieted down, and she became aware of the possibility of being with her emotions in a new way. The phrase that came to her was, "There's space for that." Confusion, upset, panic about not knowing what to do? There's space for that.

It was a phrase that resonated deeply with me, and it perfectly applied to my own experience. The sadness and loss that had been hanging around at the edges of my awareness? There is space for that. Before I wasn't ready and even enjoyed the idea of connecting to my mother through grieving. But now there is a shift. There's space for the emotions and whatever else wants to come.

As I settle into the being aware of meditation, resistance falls away. I can feel how I've subtly turned away from these feelings, and now they are welcome in a great expansive space. There's no dramatic insight or explosion of light. But there's a sense of ease that comes as the doing of resistance ends, and the feelings themselves become softer and more diffuse. The sadness is sweet, and rather than being lost in my own story of loss, surprisingly, the connection with my mother is alive and joyful.

No matter how pure our intentions to be free, the events of life can catch us off guard. Without realizing it, we create division—between life as it's actually unfolding and our stories about it, between awareness and our feelings, between what others are doing and what we want them to do.

But at any moment, when the time is right, it's always possible to bring space to that. We put down the fight, and rather than letting anything go, we let it all come in, welcoming things just as they are.

PRACTICE: *There's nothing you're supposed to do and no way that you're supposed to be. But if you feel inclined, experiment with bringing space to your experience.*

Have you been subtly pushing away feelings? Is there anything you've been resisting? Take a few minutes to slow down and be quiet. Settle into the space of just being. Let all division dissolve.

42

Two Steps to Freedom

If you leave your inner world unexplored, you end up living what seems to be a real life with real problems. But here's what is actually happening: you're living a confused and distorted version of reality.

Everything you experience is a projection of your mindset. If your mind is uncluttered by ideas and beliefs, then you'll be able to see things clearly, with nothing in the way. You'll be open to everything with no need to avoid or defend. Your mind is spacious and open, available to receive things just as they are.

But if you're not familiar with the contents of your mind, you'll project your mindset onto your experience. Your view will be shaped by your beliefs and expectations, and you'll feel separate, limited, unbalanced, and ill at ease.

Say you completely buy into the belief that you're not worthy of being loved and appreciated by others. This is your reality—that who you are is the one who is lacking whatever it takes to be part of the human race.

You look out onto the world, which includes yourself, others, and situations you find yourself in, through a veil of thinking that assumes you'll never feel that sense of belonging—because you're just too damaged to be worthy of it.

If this is your predominant belief system, there is no way you'll be able to see things clearly. Because everything you experience is filtered through this veil of the belief in your unworthiness.

- You'll show up in situations with body language that tells others you're longing and needy.

- You'll have difficulty being quiet and alone.

- You'll accept mediocrity—or worse—in your relationships and career choices.

And this is how it works for all unexplored belief systems—living in the fear that you'll fail, believing the world is against you, assuming you won't be able to cope if you turn toward your feelings.

Whatever thoughts you've taken to be true get projected onto your life experience and become your living reality that can never bring you fulfillment and satisfaction.

But there's an alternative to living with blinders on, and it involves two beautiful, sacred steps that set you free.

First, study your mind so you know how it works. What do you believe to be true that isn't? What are the filters that color your view of reality? Know what beliefs overshadow your experience of life so you can catch them.

Second—and this is the radical step—don't make these beliefs your reality. Don't touch the contents of your thoughts. Stay rooted in the presence of this now moment, and let everything unfold from here. As a friend recently discovered, "I can just be here without believing those thought patterns, and it feels good."

You can choose to live in the problems of the unexplored mind—or not. Get to know the beliefs that cause you trouble and how they project out onto the world. Then put them down and leave them. Here you are vibrant, openhearted, and fully available to life.

PRACTICE: *Apply the two steps to freedom to your own experience. First, make a list of the beliefs you hold onto that limit your view of reality and undermine your happiness. Acknowledge how each of these beliefs projects onto your relationships and circumstances to define your experience of life.*

Now go through each one. Close your eyes, and let the beliefs fall away. Put them down and let them be, giving them no interest whatsoever. Open your eyes with a spacious, uncluttered mind and clear seeing. How does this feel? Let this experience absorb into every part of your being.

Repeat with each belief every time it catches your attention.

43

Freedom from the Grip of Thought

When you hear someone tell you not to believe your thoughts, it's easier said than done. After all, it feels like you've been thinking your whole life. And aren't your thoughts integral to your existence?

Actually, no. And when we finish this analysis, you'll have an entirely different perspective.

Thoughts have many functions. They describe, judge, evaluate, and tell all kinds of stories about the present, past, and future. Some thoughts are helpful and creative. Without thinking, how would you bake your favorite cookies or plan a vacation?

But it's the distressing ones—the ones that leave you feeling sad and ill-at-ease—that deserve further investigation.

We're sometimes asked to consider if the content of a thought is true. Is it true that you're inadequate or that you'll never find a satisfying relationship?

But to fully understand thought—and to realize

the wisdom of questioning our thoughts—we need to go deeper beyond determining if the content of a thought is true or not. We need to look at the very nature of thought itself.

A thought is a mental construction that floats through the mind. It's made up of sounds or images that we give meaning to. The problem with thoughts is not that they appear. The problem is that we assume their meaning is true. So let's examine that assumption. Does a thought really mean what we assume it means?

When we were learning language as children, we were taught to associate a sound with a particular meaning. Say I ask you to visualize a pine tree. The chances are very good that your pine tree will be similar to mine. Why? We both have learned that the sounds "pine tree" refer to a green triangular shape with a brown woody stem at the bottom.

In reality, the words "pine tree" mean nothing. We might as well call that green triangle and brown stem a doorknob or an airplane. But through association and repetition, we've learned what "pine tree" means.

Language consists of these shared meanings, and it's a beautiful convention for living in the world. It's so lovely that we can describe, create, dream, and communicate with one another.

But when we take random sounds and believe they describe us, and when the meaning of those sounds is negative, false, and limiting, we're suffering unnecessarily. We're assuming that a thought is absolutely true when in fact it's not.

Consider the thought, "I am inadequate." What does that mean? I...am...inadequate. Like all mental chatter, these words are just sounds we've learned to associate with a given meaning. Put any thought to the test, especially the unpleasant ones that seem to recycle endlessly. You'll see that the meaning of the words is arbitrary—because it is.

Memories that describe what happened to you when you were young...thoughts that make you feel lacking compared to others... Just for a moment, forget what these words mean. The sounds might be present floating in your mind, but they have no impact because they mean nothing.

This understanding is utterly profound. Thoughts have a relative reality that lets us communicate, but they have no real meaning in and of themselves. So right now you can give up believing any thought that disrupts you.

If thoughts aren't true, what is? You need to go outside your mind to know. It's what's here right in this moment...the pure aliveness of being.

PRACTICE: *Experiment with discovering the truth about thoughts. Forget what the words mean, and see if they define you. Go beyond your mind, and discover the immediacy of this now moment.*

44

When Times Are Tough

No one gets a pass on life's challenges. No matter how kind you are, no matter how clean your diet or how beautiful your downward dog looks, challenges will come your way. It's the nature of life.

Our loved ones become ill, our parents pass away, friends come and go, partners leave…life is filled with happenings that invite us to dive deep into experiencing our full humanity.

Without our consent, we've embarked on a journey to somehow deal with what's been given to us. Often, our initial response is a resounding, "No!" No, not this. I don't want it this way. It's too painful. How will I go on?

This resistance serves for a while as it keeps us from feeling the depth of the feelings that are present. It gives us some time to adjust to the reality of the situation.

Even though you may be fighting what's happening with every ounce of your being, know this:

something else is present. There's an underlying flow of life that isn't agitated, no matter how agitated you are. It's not sad or disbelieving. It lovingly embraces everything that arises.

Although the surface may be extremely stormy, the depth is still and unmoving.

This understanding invites you to open to all of your experience, even resistance. I recently sat with a friend in her last days. Distressed, she said to me, "But I'm not ready yet!" I told her there's no need to be ready if she isn't. I offered her the possibility of being right where she is in not being ready. And that brought a sense of ease. She had found her way to stillness in that moment.

Being right where you are, especially with strong feelings, may be so challenging that all you want to do is avoid. It's okay to avoid your feelings for a while (but try not to be too self-destructive about it). Don't be concerned with the big picture of what's going on. Instead, stay close to the moment and check in to see what you need. And when there's more space for reflection, begin to turn toward the feelings and allow them to be.

Tough times offer us an essential teaching. We're not in control of what happens. Our personal desires and preferences have little to do with what we actually get. And in the end, blaming doesn't help, but acceptance does. Not resignation, but a deep acceptance of the reality of things.

We let ourselves be enriched by pain. And we realize the pain is not ours alone. Boundaries between others and ourselves become transparent, and we meet all of life in tenderness and love.

PRACTICE: *Whenever you go through tough times, don't rush the process. Check in often to see what you need, and make sure you have support. Don't hesitate to connect with a professional counselor. And don't worry about jumping to a spiritual understanding of what's going on. Honor and respect the humanity of your experience because that's what will be calling you.*

In the beginning, be attentive to your needs for self-care, which include basics such as eating, sleeping, and a little exercise. Make space to express your feelings.

Then, when the time is right, begin to reflect. With great self-compassion, see if you can make sense of what happened.

- *Is there anything to learn about your attachments and triggers?*

- *What do you discover when you open your heart to all that is present?*

- *What is revealed when you take the perspective of the timeless space of pure awareness?*

- *What seeds are being planted that want to sprout into the light?*

45

Fear or Love

Fear or love…fear or love… This is always our essential choice.

So let's raise our awareness about the possibility of choosing what we really, really want. Because if we're caught in conditioning, we're running on automatic programming, and we're not available to love.

We're often not aware when fear is in charge, but here are the clues. Hijacked by fear, you feel separate from others and your own experience. Your nervous mind is preoccupied by keeping you safe in a world that feels confusing and out of control. With your body in knots, you compulsively try to figure out how to get what you want to make everything okay.

Sound familiar?

It's helpful to understand that fear is built into the physical body. Since the body is designed for survival at all costs, it's loaded with inborn systems that prepare you to fight or flee when you feel threatened.

This set-up serves animals being chased in the African grasslands, but the same heightened physiology in your nervous system wears you down when you fear rejection, failure, and abandonment.

Caught in this chronic conditioned reaction, the world looks like a dangerous place. You're left *trying to* protect, defend, avoid, and cling so you can find a way to be peaceful. It's an exhausting life fueled by fear.

Seeing through the eyes of truth, we realize that this fear-based personal self we think we are is a constantly changing array of thoughts, sense perceptions, emotions, and physical sensations. You are not a fear-based animal, and you don't need all this fear to survive. In fact without out it, you might discover that you begin to thrive in beautiful and unexpected ways.

The invitation offered to you is to relax. Just for a moment, you're welcome to stop, let all the trying go, and be. Don't do anything as it dawns on you that the flow of life is here, continuously unfolding, whether you're fearful or not.

As you release into the flow, you notice peace, stillness, happiness, and simple acceptance of everything. All that you are looking for is already here.

It now comes naturally to take a friendly, loving attitude toward any sources of pain and confusion, be they people, situations, or your own feelings. No longer resisting, there's space for compassion, understanding, and the deepest intimacy.

Separation lives on fear and is guaranteed to keep

you fragmented and dissatisfied. But know this: there is another way. It's the way aligned with truth and with the fullness of life. It's the way of love.

PRACTICE: *Recognize how fear moves you, then experiment with choosing another way, which is trusting life. What happens when you're moved by love? How do you feel in your body? How does your mind feel? What do you want to do or say?*

Over and over, whenever fear arises, notice the option to choose love.

46

The Ten-Second Love Affair

Sometimes I'm blown away by the immediacy of love. I'm caught up in some story in my mind, then the thought arises reminding me to consider the other person. I'm deliberating about a decision from the perspective of what would be right for me, then I'm astounded by the shift in awareness tapping me on the shoulder that naturally takes into account everyone and everything involved. For no reason, joy bubbles up everywhere.

These are divine moments when the truth of being shines through. Stories are held lightly. Problems fall away. The ideas of past and future have no meaning. We can't make these moments happen, but we can celebrate when they arrive.

The ten-second love affair. It's closer than close and changes everything. It opens our eyes, explodes our hearts open, and shakes us awake to forget the illusion of a divided world and melt into love.

Try it right now. Can you drop all the suffering and love this moment?

- Can you love that knot in your stomach?

- Can you embrace the wrinkles on your face like a long-lost friend?

- Can you stand before that guy who irks you with the laser vision to meet *his* suffering with love?

Expanding deeply into these sacred moments of connection, the distinction between this and that disappears. The ideas of me and other are insignificant.

All form burns in the sacred fire of love, revealing emptiness sweeter than you could ever imagine. The heart can't stop singing a song of celebration. Finally, you're free!

PRACTICE: *Experience your own ten-second love affair. Just do it—right now!*

47

Oh, This...

Oh, this...It's a simple phrase that can change everything. In no time at all, "Oh, this" will radically alter your perspective.

When does "Oh, this" come into play? Whatever happens, whatever arises, the most simple and intelligent response is, "Oh, this." It means you accept, you embrace, you receive what's here with an open mind and heart. Say "Oh, this" to:

- What's happening right now in your present circumstances

- Memories of things that occurred in the past

- Things people say and do

- Your own emotional reactions

Oh, this is not at all about being passive and resigned. It's not about gritting your teeth and putting up with or getting through. You don't have to grin and bear it. And it doesn't keep you from intelligently saying no when the clarity comes to do so.

"Oh, this" says a full-hearted "Yes!" to what is right now. Then you can see things clearly and not through the veil of your personal wishes that want them to be different than they are. The sense of your individual self retreats, and you're one with the unfolding of life in this moment.

Say that someone gets on your nerves. When that happens to me, I feel the frustration rising and the desire to snap back or shut down. I'm totally in resistance, wanting them to stop doing the thing that bothers me.

What short-circuits the problem is the simple deeply-felt phrase, "Oh, this." With my mind, body, and heart I say, "Oh, this" to the frustration I feel, the urge to say something unkind, the other's actions. Immediately, reactivity ends and I melt into the deepest acceptance. Now there's space for compassion and clear seeing.

Many of us are way more familiar with "Not this," than "Oh, this." Consider these:

- I don't *want* you to be saying that.

- I don't *want* this to be happening.

- That *shouldn't* have happened.

- I don't *want* to feel the way I feel.

These statements are all about resisting. How often do you not want to feel what you're actually feeling? How often do you long to revise history or write the script for what you think should happen now and in the future? And how much pain do these reactions bring to your life?

What I love more than anything is that there is always a way to discover peace—because it's here as our true nature, the ever-present ground of being. "Oh, this" gets us out of our heads and into the full aliveness of the moment. It wakes us up to what's real.

PRACTICE: *Notice when you're resisting. You'll find clues in a busy mind swirling with pronouncements about how things are supposed to be and a body filled with tension.*

Now simply glide through your awareness the simple phrase, "Oh, this." Feel it deeply in every part of your being. Let "Oh, this" enter the nooks and crannies of your mind and the cells in your body. Let it open you beyond your personal self to the boundless nature of life as it is.

"Oh, this" is an endless practice steeped in love.

48

True Service

How many of us burn ourselves out trying to do good in the world? We think that being of service means serving others no matter what. And we end up losing our boundaries and betraying our truth while strongly believing we need to keep giving. It's an exhausting conflict that has its roots in false ideas about how we define ourselves that ultimately lead to alienation and separation.

We start out with good intentions—to express love through our actions. But soon it gets messy. We feel rejected when our help isn't received. We end up being taken advantage of. And we don't believe we're allowed to say no.

Our personal self is on the line because the results of what we do are attached to our happiness. We're not giving just for the sake of giving. We're giving so we can feel good or righteous or self-satisfied.

The problem here is the identity with the personal

self, and the solution is to know that is not who we really are.

True service emerges effortlessly with complete surrender of everything personal. We take our beliefs about ourselves and the world, our stories, our expectations and needs, our attachment to any outcomes and throw all of it into the holy fire of truth. Because these are ideas created in our minds and none of them can begin to define the truth of who we are.

True service is revealed as simply listening. It's not knowing anything and being willing to be moved. It has nothing to do with thoughts or ideas. And it doesn't come from lack, need, or the wish to feel good about ourselves. Actions happen with no regard to the outcome.

At the beginning of my career as a psychotherapist, I was confused about service. I felt frustrated when clients didn't improve and considered that maybe my skills were inadequate. I'm so grateful for the help that changed my perspective entirely.

With no personal needs involved, I could show up fully in every moment. Without attachment to outcomes, the joy of doing this work blossomed. All that is being asked is complete surrender, and all that is left is emptiness and love. How that looks is none of my business.

True service is not only about how we relate to others. Every moment of surrender and listening is service. In these temporary human forms, we're in service to the undivided, to the flow of life, to how love wants to move. And it takes into account everyone and everything. It's the energy you bring to driving in a traffic jam, the way you chop the celery, the kindest "no" that speaks what's true.

Do you want to truly be of service? Then know who you're not and discover who you are.

PRACTICE: *Reflect on the idea of being of service with these questions. Consider each one and simply let the answers come.*

- *How do I get stuck around the idea of being of service to others?*

- *What beliefs do I hold that make me want to give to others?*

- *Do I serve others out of fear, lack, or a sense of inadequacy?*

- *Am I looking for approval or acknowledgment?*

- *What makes it difficult for me to say no?*

- *How would it feel to surrender the need to serve?*

- *Can I forget everything and let myself be moved?*

49

The Paradox of
Following Your Heart

Okay, now we're going to get real. Because I've recently been contemplating what it means to follow your heart, and I've realized that it's not a simple undertaking.

Say you're in a loveless, antagonistic marriage raising two young children. Your heart tells you to leave—and to stay for the benefit of your kids. Or you've found "the one," but she's of a different culture or religion, and you know that your parents will be tremendously disappointed when they find out about your choice.

Following your heart would be a whole lot simpler if other people didn't suffer from the consequences of your actions.

From the perspective of the absolute truth of reality, which is the unifying ground of love, none of this matters. The universe is only moving itself around. But, as humans, the circumstances we're in take center stage. Should we suppress our true desires so we don't rock the boat? Is meeting others' needs the right thing to do? It feels real and seems important.

How to live that paradox between knowing we're universal consciousness and living our humanity is an engaging question. And it's way more about living the question than knowing the answers.

We start from a position of not knowing. Not knowing what to do, not trusting the mind or emotions to tell us. We acknowledge our personal concerns, then surrender them as we let ourselves be guided and moved.

We trust in the remembrance that all beings, regardless of how deluded they seem to be in their actions and thinking, are expressions of the one source that can't be separate from itself. This means that we wisely open to how everyone and everything is impacted.

And we listen deeply to allow space for the voice of truth to be heard.

Now, here is the fierce part. We let go of any ideas about how things should look. Should I leave my marriage? Should I put my family at risk to embark on my own dreams? Should I risk failure, ridicule, or rejection for what I know is true?

Many lives have been lived in fear and limitation and others have pushed the edges in every way imaginable despite the potential consequences. Neither of these is right nor wrong.

Truth cuts through to what is real, and love and compassion invite an unbounded opening to the whole. Here, following our hearts has fresh meaning. It's not about our personal desires—and it is. Any given situation doesn't matter—and it does. We strive to find peace—yet peace is already our nature.

We welcome the messy multiplicity of life held in the stillness and silence of being.

PRACTICE*: When considering how or if to follow your heart, reflect on these questions:*

- *What if I put aside my personal desires? Not that you should, but what happens when you do?*

- *What do I realize when I feel into each person's experience of the situation?*

- *What am I attached to?*

- *What am I willing to risk?*

- *Can I welcome any emotions that appear?*

- *What ideas do I hold about how things should look? What if I let them go and open to not knowing?*

- *Can I let things be messy?*

- *Standing as the ground of being, what do I notice?*

50

Finish with the Past— It's Time

Iknow exactly what it's like to be stuck on resentments from the past, because that was my experience for many years. I remember I was in my late 20's when a friend said to me, "Gosh, you talk about your parents a lot!" And now I want to say to her that I'm so sorry I bored you with all that drama!

You don't realize how much these hooks affect you and those around you until you're free of them. When you still have unfinished business, it consumes your thought processes, dominates your feelings, and saps your energy. And you're looking at life from the perspective of being wounded or victimized.

Try it out right now to understand how the past affects you. Pretend you're looking through a thin veil of fabric. You can see everything out there, but not at all clearly. Now imagine that the fabric is the mindset that there's something wrong with you or that you're a victim of circumstances. How do you view people, your relationships, your opportunities? What do you think about? How do you feel?

I'm guessing you're becoming keenly aware of the limits of this way of being.

From where I sit now, I can tell you that it's really, really wonderful to be free of the past. It's not that memories or emotional reactions never appear, but it doesn't matter to me if they do. When I feel them try to grab me, I turn instead toward light and freedom as they slip away into oblivion. Then I'm freed up to be fully present with whatever experience is right here in this moment.

Finishing with the past usually takes attention, time, and patience. I know the phrase tells us that time heals all wounds. But I've sat with many people in their 70's and 80's who are still feeling pain and wishing things could have been different.

Some of us are dealing with what psychiatrist and author Mark Epstein calls "the trauma of everyday life" and others have had some pretty nasty things happen. The events that happened are finished, but they're kept alive in your mind, emotions, and body. It serves no one, especially yourself, to continue to be dragged down by these events.

At this point, I can hear you asking, "Yes, but how do I finish with the past? I've tried everything, but I'm still stuck." Here's the most important thing about getting started.

You need to give this problem your full attention for as long as it takes. Unfinished business from the past has to do with how it lives in you now. So it requires bringing your attention to your experience and owning it—what stories you're taking to be true about yourself and others and the feelings these stories stir up. If you keep blaming others, I promise you, you'll stay stuck forever.

When I realized that the resentments I held onto were hurting me more than anyone else, frankly, it was easy to let them go.

Take responsibility for your own healing. And want peace within yourself more than anything.

PRACTICE: *In your own quiet moments, shift your attention to witnessing your story, like you're an audience member watching it playing out on the stage. Now, more objective, feel the suffering of everyone involved so you can understand what actually happened—not just the events, but what was behind them. So much compassion for so much pain…*

Then directly address your thoughts about what should and shouldn't have happened. If you keep giving life to these, they will derail your good intentions for peace. What happened happened. Accept this deeply, which means you can no longer avoid the feelings hiding out in the recesses of unconsciousness.

Take a deep breath, and lean in. Peek beyond your fears and defenses into the tender spaces inside you that need your love. Open your heart to the longings, disappointments, and sorrows and welcome them in. Love them fully and deeply. Let this be your practice whenever these feelings arise.

As the witness and the welcoming presence, you're the safe haven of awareness that allows everything. This is what heals division so you can realize that you've always been whole and completely at peace.

51

Free of the Anxious Mind

Several years ago I was milling about in the court-yard outside a yoga studio waiting for a weekend training to start. I struck up a conversation with the woman next to me, and her part went something like this: "How many people will be in the class? Do you think we'll get a break? I wonder if I'll be able to do the yoga. Do you think the instructor will be good at answering questions?"

I stood there mostly in silence with great compassion for her suffering because there it was, on full display, the pain of the anxious mind.

If you take a look at her questions, what is the answer? I don't know. There was no way I could know how many people will be in the class or what was going to be presented. These questions are all fear-based expressions of a mind completely uncomfortable with not knowing.

When our attention is hijacked by the anxious

mind, we're separate from the flow of life. We're caught in judgments, expectations, and fearful projections into the future. And our life experience is filled with worry and confusion. These thoughts feed agitation in the mind and body, and keep us under constant surveillance of the world out there to make sure we're safe and protected.

How can we possibly be joyful if the anxious mind is in charge?

I used to live in the land of the anxious mind. I would get overwhelmed at the drop of a hat. I've walked away from a basket full of stuff in a store because I was too anxious to continue shopping. And I've missed many opportunities for friendship with wonderful people because I was too scared to connect. I know what it's like to peer out from behind a wall of anxious thinking making me terrified of walking into a yoga training.

And I'm deeply grateful to the teachers who guided me to recognize how much fear was behind my suffering. Because that was the starting point of a rich and fruitful journey to realizing that the peace I was aching for was already here. Calling it anxiety kept me locked in my mind, but applying the label of fear helped my attention expand to include the body.

The journey began by being conscious of my in-the-moment experience of fearful thoughts and jittery bodily sensations. And it evolved into the continual realization that none of these thoughts accurately describes my identity or my perception of events.

I notice some underlying fear now and then, for example, when I'm about to speak in front of a large group of people. But that everyday fear? It's rarely here.

If you're caught by your anxious mind, you don't need to work to improve or change one thing about your thoughts or yourself. You don't need to stop your mind or come up with more optimistic thoughts.

But you do need to become aware. Commit to being aware of your in-the-moment experience. Do that deeply, and here's what you'll discover. At the core of your experience, prior to any thoughts or feelings, you're conscious and alive. Thoughts may appear in you, but they're made-up ideas that can't touch your beauty. Being stuck in an anxious mind is optional, as freedom is always here with a simple shift of attention to what is true and real.

PRACTICE: *Anxiety is deeply held in the mind and body, so be devoted to finding freedom from it.*

Once a day or more often, sit quietly and create a huge open space for the sensations in your body to come to awareness. There's no goal with this practice. Just sit, breathe, and be, and let all the sensations come and go.

Learn to recognize fearful thoughts. At times when you feel anxious, notice what your thoughts are saying and how they pull your attention away from the moment. These thoughts are never true about reality.

Remember that what you pay attention to is what flourishes. Think anxious thoughts, and you're sure to feel more anxious. Instead, as much as possible, shift your attention to the space of awareness.

When you're opening to physical sensations, be aware of the awareness itself rather than the sensations. When you let go of thoughts, let your attention rest in itself. Rather than focusing on objects like thoughts and sensations, be the boundless space of aware presence.

52

Being Who You Are

We humans are experts at pretending we don't know who we are. We're experts at living the lies we tell ourselves—that we're limited and inadequate, that we're broken beyond repair, that our judgments of others and ourselves are true.

But what about living the truth of who you really are? When you investigate deeply, you'll discover that your true nature has nothing to do with limitation. You are infinitely loving, overflowing with possibility, and impossible to contain. You are the brilliance that lights up everything.

And in your heart of hearts, you know this is true.

Everyone and everything you encounter manifests from the one source: pure awareness. This means that at its essence, nothing is separate from anything else. See a tree? It arises from the same source as you. Stand before another person? At the source, there aren't two people, just life unfolding. Let the one heart be illuminated as the freshness of the moment moves you.

Why not stop pretending, and be who you are. Living this truth, the way of happiness and peace, is not "spiritual." It's practical, tangible, and available to you right now.

PRACTICE: *Try this simple experiment. Consciously be who you are. In any moment, give up your personal agendas and dissolve into the effortless flow of life. Be a welcoming, receptive host who is at peace with whatever arises.*

Regardless of what your thoughts tell you, life flows seamlessly. Lose the illusion of the separate self and be one with the flow.

Be who you are—aligned with the fullness of life that is open, boundless, peaceful, and free.

To learn more and to contact Gail,
please visit **http://GailBrenner.com/**
where you'll find hundreds of free articles,
videos, and information about private sessions.

Like her Facebook page for daily inspiration.
https://www.facebook.com/gailbrennerdotcom

When you sign up to receive notices
of new articles and events,
you'll receive a download of the first chapter of
The End of Self-Help:
Discovering Peace and Happiness
Right at the Heart of Your Messy, Scary, Brilliant Life.

http://gailbrenner.com/email-signup/

REVIEWS

If you enjoyed this book, please consider
leaving a review on Amazon to let others know.
Even a brief review is gratefully appreciated.

About the Author

Gail Brenner, Ph.D. is the author of *The End of Self-Help: Discovering Peace and Happiness Right at the Heart of Your Messy, Scary, Brilliant Life*, available on Amazon.com. She is a clinical psychologist, author, and speaker who joyfully helps people discover that suffering is optional—and a lover of truth with a fire that burns brightly.

Gail has worked with clients for over 20 years, bringing laser-like clarity to the confusion of common human problems, such as reactive emotions, feelings of personal inadequacy, and relationship struggles. She skillfully unravels distorted identities people take to be true and guides them to discover and live from their true essence that is already whole, peaceful, and at ease.

Gail has trained primary care physicians to address psychosocial issues in their patients and has special expertise working with older adults and their families, bringing clear seeing and compassion to the transitions of aging, death, and dying. She has published numerous professional articles on coping with stress and chronic medical illness.

19367869R00099

Printed in Great Britain
by Amazon